LET'S GROW

ON THE NORTHERN PRAIRIE

Other books by Eric Bergeson:

Down on the Farm
Still on the Farm
Off the Farm
Back on the Farm
Pirates on the Prairie
A Treasury of Old Souls
Successful Gardening on the Northern Prairie

LET'S GROW

ON THE NORTHERN PRAIRIE

ERIC BERGESON

Country Scribe Publishing
4177 County Highway 1
Fertile, MN 56540
ericbergeson.com

Cover and interior design by Lance Thorn

Printed in USA.

First Edition, 2019

ISBN 978-1-64713-166-1

ABOUT THE AUTHOR

Eric Bergeson has spent his entire life as a part of Bergeson Nursery, a business started by his grandfather Melvin Bergeson near Fertile, Minnesota in 1936. Eric owned Bergeson Nursery for seventeen years. Over the past twenty years, Eric has spoken to hundreds of groups about the joys and challenges of gardening on the northern prairie. His book Successful Gardening on the Northern Prairie has sold over 15,000 copies. Let's Grow is Eric's eighth book, and his second about landscaping and gardening.

ACKNOWLEDGEMENTS

I am grateful to my father, Paul, and brother, Joe, for their input and suggestions, as well as my mother, Glenda, for her unwavering support.

My sister, Tracie Bergeson, managed the book project and brought it to publication. Finally, thanks to my partner, Lance, for his patience and artistic talents as the designer of the book's layout.

—Eric Bergeson, November 2019

INDEX OF ARTICLES

A SUMMER TOUR...

Members of the Madison, SD, garden club with the author at the Madison city

To my pleasant surprise, Successful Gardening on the Northern Prairie's audience spread beyond our customers at Bergeson Nursery in Fertile, MN, to include gardeners on the prairies of all of North and South Dakota, Montana, and western Minnesota down to the Iowa border.

Our situation across this vast terrain is much the same: Zone 3-4 temperatures with nearly constant wind, as well as alkaline soils. Although each locale has specific challenges and opportunities, more unites us than divides us, making it possible to lay out the basics of northern prairie horticulture for the layperson in a single volume.

However, as much as I loved reaching a broader audience than planned, I felt sheepish claiming expertise in vast swaths of territory I had never visited.

New Rockford, ND, on a hot afternoon: the lady seated second from the front on the right is 90 years old and has been sneaking ammonium sulphate out of the farm supply for use on her garden for decades.

To address that deficiency, I set about to tour the region in 2019.

After completing a ten-town tour of libraries in Northwestern Minnesota in April at the generous behest of the Lake Agassiz Regional Library system, I stole LARL's idea and toured 55 towns in North Dakota during the month of June.

After the first weeks of the North Dakota tour went well, I added South Dakota for the month of July.

By the time the tour ended on a perfect evening at the picnic shelter in beautiful McKennan Park in Sioux Falls, I had spoken 114 times, met hundreds of wonderful people, toured hundreds of towns, scanned thousands of miles of countryside—and was tuckered out!

To be sure, I was neither Lewis nor Clark. I stayed in cushy hotels and ate well, thanks to all those small-town Subways, repeated visits to the Applebees in Jamestown and Watertown, and great local restaurants such as McTwist in Wishek, ND, the C & N Cafe in Hettinger, ND, and Pereboom's in Webster, SD. The highlight of local dining was the prime rib at the Wrangler Inn in Mobridge, SD, done perfectly and eaten with a stunning A-framed view of the Missouri River and the unseasonably green bluffs opposite.

Why are these people smiling? Their town, Walhalla, ND, suffered more winter damage to their trees and shrubs than any other I saw on the tour. Perhaps it's that they are still surrounded by one of the most forested areas on the northern prairie, the beautiful Pembina Gorge.

Prairie weather added its drama. About twenty of us squeezed into a gazebo in Rugby, ND, during a much-needed downpour. A lady interrupted my talk as thunder rumbled around us in Rapid City: "Would you please not lean on that pole while it is lightning?"

Several city parks in South Dakota, from Flandreau in the east to Sturgis in the west, were flooded, requiring adjustments in scheduling, word of which didn't always reach all of those who hoped to attend.

The first arrival for a morning talk at the city park in Beach, ND, approaches beneath an old-time silver poplar.

The day I was slated to give five talks in towns surrounding Sioux Falls started with a talk in Brandon under threatening skies, and followed with talks in Canton, Harrisburg and Beresford, towns which had sustained 70-mile-per-hour wind damage only hours before.

A perfect day to sit on the lawn in front of the bandshell in Garrison, ND.

A Saturday morning talk in Bismarck started at 53° F. The rain stopped just in time for the talk in Grafton. Same for Devils Lake, but it was still cool and wet, and the Twins were playing, so I was thrilled to see so many people on a night more suited for a recliner, an afghan, and a little Bomba ball.

Thanks to the Red Door Art Gallery in Wahpeton for hosting the final stop on the first day of the Successful Gardening on the Northern Prairie North Dakota tour!

The Northern Plains Botanic Garden Society in Fargo generously hosted in their greenhouse in north Fargo. Members provided muffins and coffee, plus somebody brought 40 pastries! All available calories disappeared on the cool, wet Saturday.

The Milbank Chamber of Commerce hosted my talk in their stunning new Visitor's Center, and helped draw in a nice crowd on yet another wet June afternoon.

It was so windy in Gettysburg, SD, that the library offered up its community room at the last minute. The park I was assigned in Belfield, ND, had a tiny picnic shelter, and it was pouring, so a lady volunteered the pavilion downtown, posted it on Facebook three minutes before the talk was to start, and we had a nice crowd. The wonders of social media!

Rain threatened at the uncovered amphitheater in Ipswich, SD, so we moved to a little shelter across the street to discuss Edmunds County's extremely difficult growing conditions, with some attendees standing in a steady drizzle for over an hour.

I had considered touring cities in eastern Montana during August, but by the time I finished South Dakota, the hotels were blurring together, I knew which sinks didn't work in every rest area on I-94, I-29 and I-90, and I had put 18,000 miles on my car.

However, I was honored that several Montana gardeners, including the Glendive garden club, showed up to talks in western North Dakota. I hope to get to Montana soon!

I was happy to speak over the roar of the rain-
swollen Split Rock River going over the dam in

I learned from the experienced gardeners who attended, and I learned as I drove from town to town, and around town. The more lost I got trying to find the city park, the more I learned!

By the end, my head was full of experiences and ideas. I decided to put them in a second gardening book, this one with pictures.

WHAT IS THE NORTHERN PRAIRIE?

For our purposes, all of North Dakota and most of South Dakota are northern prairie, with Vermillion and Yankton, SD, included on an honorary basis, provided their citizens don't gloat about their warmer winter temperatures and ability to grow exotic trees such as sycamore.

Western Minnesota's sprawling Seventh Congressional District as it is presently gerrymandered coincides almost perfectly with the portion of the state considered northern prairie.

Massive Montana contains plenty of northern prairie east of the Rockies. Once you get above 3,000 feet in elevation, however, the rules change. The sunlight is more intense, first and last frost dates less predictable, and there is more frequent hail—which leads higher elevation gardeners to cover their vegetable garden with two layers of chicken netting in hopes of slowing the falling ice chunks before they tear apart the tomatoes!

For the purposes of horticulture, the region considered the northern prairie shares Zone 3 and 4 winter temperatures, as well as predominantly, sometimes extremely, alkaline soils.

THE YELLOW ROSES OF BEACH

As I searched for Beach, ND's city park on a sunny morning in late June, I spotted a specimen of the old Yellow Rose of Texas in full bloom in a long-abandoned yard.

What a sight! I had to pull over to take a picture.

A block further on, there was another. Another stop. Another picture.

Soon, I realized that if I stopped for every yellow rose blooming in Beach, I would never make it to the park to speak!

17

A ROSE WITH A PAST

The history of the Yellow Rose of Texas (Rosa foetida) in western culture goes back to the 1500s, when it was brought to southern Europe from Persia. Europe had no yellow roses at the time, and Rosa foetida provided genetics for many new hybrids.

European immigrants brought the rose to the United States, where, unlike other rose breeds, it showed an actual preference for the prairies of the west. Indeed, stands of yellow roses can still be found along the old Oregon Trail.

In 1830, George Harison, a lawyer, found what he thought to be an improved sport of the original Rosa foetida in his garden in Manhattan. He introduced the selection as "Harison's Yellow."

Harison's Yellow is taller and more vigorous than the species, which is now referred to as Persian Yellow. The Harison's flowers, though more numerous, are smaller and slightly more pale than the Persian.

To the present, despite the introduction of thousands of more popular rose varieties in the intervening 200 years, the Persian Yellow and Harison's Yellow have maintained a small niche in the rose market, if only as a sort of historical curiosity.

Both versions of the Yellow Rose of Texas are listed as hardy to Zone 4. However, I have seen healthy specimens in Grand Forks, which is Zone 3. At our nursery, also in Zone 3, both the Harison's Yellow and Persian Yellow have lasted years, but at times have frozen back.

A Persian Yellow rose in Beach, ND

18

REVIVING THE TRADITION

I just spent two days trying to get rid of that thing!" said an exasperated gardener who showed up at the talk in Bismarck.

Familiar with the thorns involved, I was sympathetic with his plight.

Then I realized: The very best way of getting a new Yellow Rose of Texas is by stealing a sucker from a big mother plant. The man had just thrown hundreds of starters of a valuable plant that nurseries hesitate to produce!

Most big wholesale nurseries prefer to raise hardy roses from cuttings, and that just doesn't work well with the Yellow Rose of Texas.

But there is a solution which merely requires ingenuity, neighborliness, and a few scratches on one's arms—things which shouldn't bother a northern prairie gardener.

To successfully establish a Yellow Rose of Texas in a new location, a shoot stolen from around the mother rose's base need only have a little root and a little top. Cut back the top to one foot or a little less to allow the root to develop first.

Stealing suckers is the method our ancestors used to bring the Yellow Rose of Texas to the northern prairie. They stole shoots from dormant plants back east, wrapped them carefully, kept them damp throughout the months-long journey, and transplanted them in their new digs out west.

Yet another Persian Yellow rose in Beach, ND

A Harison's Yellow at the Community United Church in Beach, ND.

A ROSE NEARLY FORGOTTEN

So why did the Yellow Rose of Texas, so valued by the early settlers, fall into obscurity?

•It only blooms once, in early summer.

•The Yellow Rose of Texas shrub gets rangy, and is a little big for urban lots.

•It has really nasty thorns!

•It is difficult for nurseries to reproduce with their traditional methods.

•In more humid climes, it is subject to leaf disease.

•The Yellow Rose of Texas is not a tea rose. Tea roses have dominated public's perception of what a rose should be like for the past 100 years.

•Finally, the Yellow Rose of Texas suckers, which merely means it sends out shoots from the base and gets ever wider over the years.

NEIGHBOR HELPING NEIGHBOR...

Two days after I heard the Bismarck gardener's tale of woe, a gardener in Mott, ND, expressed frustration at the increasing size of her Harison's Yellow rose. Seconds later, somebody in the back row shouted, "Where can I get one?"

Two problems with a solution right under our nose!

I suggested that Gardener 1 get in touch with Gardener 2. Sure enough, they already knew each other.

It is my hope that next spring, Gardener 1 will allow Gardener 2 to steal some shoots from her rose.

I hinted that each shoot was worth $20, but in reality I think a jar of salsa or jam would be about right.

Using good old prairie neighborliness, we can raise thousands of the Yellow Rose of Texas in our prairie yards. And we should. The ten days of bloom in June, when other flowers haven't really began to produce color, are truly memorable.

I will always remember Beach, ND, as the town with all the yellow roses—if only because I happened to come through in mid-June.

It doesn't have to be just Beach.

THE EMERALD ASH BORER INVASION
Facing the Challenge

A Landmark Under Threat...

The highway into Kindred, ND, is flanked by a walking path and a beautiful row of green ash. Shown here is a small portion of the impressive planting, which features a well-shaped green ash cultivar, likely the Patmore.

Unfortunately, Kindred will, in the coming years, face a choice: Inoculate the trees against the emerald ash borer to the tune of $100 per year per tree, or see the trees killed by the bug.

As of late 2019, the emerald ash borer has established itself in the Sioux Falls, SD, area and was recently discovered in Worthington, MN. The bug brings with it a history of total destruction of the ash trees in its path.

All of the northern prairie is in the borer's path.

The facts are grim and unambiguous: No untreated ash trees have survived an invasion of emerald ash borer. Hundreds of millions of ash trees have already died since the bug debuted on this continent in Michigan in 2002. Costs to local governments for prevention and clean-up have run into the hundreds of millions of dollars.

Dutch Elm disease, as devastating as it was, left a few living American elm in its wake, some of which remain resistant to the virus and are being reproduced.

Barring a late miracle, there is no such hope for the ash.

The emerald ash borer's impact will be outsized on the northern prairie, where green ash trees play a large role in the natural forest and cultivated landscapes.

The threat of the emerald ash borer has foisted Dr. John Ball of South Dakota State University into an unwelcome position of prominence: Dr. Ball is the region's foremost expert on the bug, and has not only traveled to Asia to study the pest's 100-year path of destruction, but has consulted broadly with experts in areas of the United States where the borer has already swept through.

Dr. Ball accurately predicted the date of the borer's arrival in Sioux Falls fifteen years in advance. His conclusions about what will happen and what is to be done are to be taken seriously.

According to Dr. Ball, the emerald ash borer will kill every ash tree on the northern prairie but for those injected with insecticide. Such injections have proven to be 100% effective, but cost an average of $100 per year per tree.

No ash trees will be left standing.

The bug is thorough in its destruction. Once the borer is finished with an ash tree, it falls over. The bug robs the wood of its strength to the point where the tree not only falls, but shatters. The falling trees pose a danger to public safety.

The city of Sioux Falls' decision to begin removing ash trees now, even some which are not yet infected, has met with some controversy. In fact, it is a necessary step.

With 87,000 ash trees, Sioux Falls and its residents will only be able to afford to save a few thousand.

As the bug accelerates its destruction, crews and budgets will be strained if their task is not spread out over several years. The time to start is now.

The strategy adopted by the city, at the advice of Dr. Ball and others, is to delay the spread of the bug as long as possible, and to spread the devastation over as many years as possible.

Local governments across the northern prairie need a similar plan.

Given the physical danger falling trees pose to the population and its property as well as the prevalence of ash trees in the landscape, every municipality on the northern prairie will confront this problem in the near future.

Northern prairie city governments must face the questions: How many ash trees can we afford to save? When do we begin to treat those we choose to keep? When should we begin to saw down the doomed trees to spread out the cost of removing them?

WHAT IS THE HOMEOWNER TO DO?

For the homeowner, the choices are simpler, if no less grim.

The first fact, and the most important: It is a waste of money to treat your trees until the borer has been detected within fifteen miles.

Do not assume that your ash is infected with the borer if it looks sick. Particularly in the Red River Valley of the north, many ash are in severe decline for a host of other reasons.

Do not accept the services of any purported inoculator who comes knocking. Each city, once the bug is detected, should maintain a list of certified, dependable and ethical arborists.

Those on that list will be so busy they won't need to hawk their services door-to-door.

We can only hope that enough people get trained to administer the treatment to keep the price at its present level.

To prepare for the bug's arrival, identify the ash on your property. Contemplate which, if any, of those ash are worth keeping at the approximate rate of $100 per year.

Saw down any ash (and there are plenty on the northern prairie the farther north you go) that already look unhealthy. Why put up with scruffy trees if they are going to die anyway?

Disease resistant American elm, such as this Princeton Elm, will be a valuable replacement for the green ash, particularly on boulevards.

And then? Wait for the emerald ash borer to arrive in your immediate locale. It could take years. It might be a decade. But when it does, you will hear about it.

The silver lining...

Ash trees aren't a very interesting tree. In fact, they're usually a little dowdy.

We now have the opportunity to replace green ash with other native tree varieties that are superior both in longevity and appearance.

Let's get busy!

A linden growing in a southern subdivision of Kindred, ND. A cultivar of linden such as this would be a good replacement for the doomed green ash along the highway between this subdivision and central Kindred.

WHAT SHOULD KINDRED DO?

Back to the situation in Kindred, with its stately row of green ash. What can be done?

There is enough land to the east of the tree row to plant a new row of trees which, one hopes, will have time to mature before the bug arrives to take the row of ash.

The question becomes, what tree to plant?

The wise choice would be to plant a mix: Basswood, oak, hackberry, cottonwood—as many different hardy varieties as are on the market. Planting a variety would protect against a future bug taking the entire row.

In this case, the wise choice is a disappointing choice. The whole point of Kindred's planting was to create a striking, impressive, and formal welcome to the city.

To preserve the dignified formality, one tree choice stands out: linden, particularly the Greenspire, a cultivar of the European linden. Proven for many decades, uniformly triangular, and free of disease, the Greenspire linden would be every bit as stately as the row of green ash.

Whatever the Kindred city fathers and mothers decide to do, they are to be congratulated for planting and maintaining the present row.

SPECIES VS. CULTIVARS

Trees purchased for planting can be divided into two groups: Either the tree is of a *species*, or they are a *cultivar* from within a species.

A tree from the *species* grew from seed, either in nature or in the nursery. Each *seed-grown* tree is genetically unique, although in most cases they all look pretty much the same, even to trained eyes.

An ornamental pear thriving in Enderlin, ND, is a fruitless and strikingly formal pear cultivar.

Cultivars require grafting, and are therefore more expensive. Cultivars have also been introduced by somebody who receives royalties, and are therefore more heavily promoted.

The market shapes which new trees gain traction, and enter production. Market forces, unfortunately, pay little heed to the needs of the sparsely-populated northern prairie.

The large urban and suburban market drives the direction of the breeding towards compactness. In our large, open spaces, we need size!

For the prairie tree planter, there may be occasional reason to purchase a *cultivar*. Most often, however, the *species* is not only as good, but better—and likely less costly.

The greatest northern prairie tree of them all, bur oak, should be planted by the ten thousands. It is sturdy. It is long-lived. It is beautiful. It has been native to the northern prairie for thousands of years.

But you will *never* see an article or advertisement promoting it. Nor will the box stores, or even some local nurseries, bother to carry it. It is planted from seed, a *species* tree, and thus makes for an uninteresting purchase.

Yet, it is the wisest purchase.

To find the plain old tree of the species, the northern prairie tree planter must be a tough, savvy and determined consumer.

It helps that we have soil and water conservation districts which specialize in selling cheap and small seedling trees of the species.

33

A PROBLEM WITH POLLINATOR PANIC ON THE PRAIRIE

Pollinators, or "beneficial insects," are in trouble world-wide, according to headlines and magazine articles. Bee colonies have disappeared, monarch butterflies can't find food or a place to lay eggs, and other beneficial insects are succumbing to the use of farm chemicals.

In response, millions have rallied to help the beleaguered bugs. Well-meaning gardeners allow milkweed, once considered a weed, to grow. You can enroll in a class on how to create a "pollinator friendly" flower garden. The Minnesota legislature got into the act by appropriating $900,000 to help people establish insect-friendly yards.

Once again, the good folks on the northern prairie have been led by the nose by the coastal media into doing what makes good sense in California and New York, but makes less sense for us.

A monarch butterfly feeds on a native echinacea on a preserved virgin prairie near Twin Valley, MN.

POLLINATOR PARADISE

Let's be clear: The northern prairie is, always has been, and likely always will be, a pollinator paradise.

North Dakota perennially leads the nation in honey production with South Dakota and Montana not far behind. Production increases annually.

Our bees are happy. And if you talk to an area bee keeper, their solution to colony die-off is, surprise, surprise: *good beekeeping.*

We have more good beekeepers on the northern prairie, if honey production is any indicator, than any other region of the country.

A FEAST FOR BUTTERFLIES

As for monarch butterflies, it is true they need common milkweed. But if my math is sound, there are more milkweed growing on the wildlife preserves and ditch banks within 10 miles of my hometown of Fertile, MN—several million plants—than we would have if every home in the state put in a pollinator garden!

Monarch butterfly counts are indeed down precipitously—in California. But in the region in Mexico where monarchs from the entire North American continent mass together during winter, numbers are not only up over the past five years, but the population has multiplied several times.

To help the pollinators on the prairie, merely plant flowers. Any flowers. All different kinds of them. Then sit back and watch our already plentiful good bugs feast on the blooms!

Why be so crass as to pull the rug out from beneath such a noble movement as the drive to help pollinators? What harm is there in encouraging people to help good bugs, even though our good bugs don't need the help?

Because we have our own big problem.

A large portion of our prairie forest, the green ash trees, is doomed by the all-destroying emerald ash borer. The ash must be replaced or the prairie will be as barren for our descendants as it was for our pioneer ancestors.

Humans have a limited amount of time and energy to do noble, nature-nurturing, big picture things. Spending that energy helping bugs who don't need help burns up hours and energy–hours and energy better spent raising and planting the trees that will shade our grandchildren on hot summer days, and shelter their homes from the brunt of winter winds.

Yes, let the milkweed grow in your garden to satisfy the urge to nurture, and to join in present trends.

But while you're at it, raise a single bur oak tree from an acorn, or small seedling. Protect the young tree from the deer until it grows large enough to be out of their reach. Fertilize, prune and nurture the oak sapling to young adulthood, after which it can be safely left to its own devices.

After just a few years, you can take credit for an important accomplishment which will leave a mark for the next 200 years or more.

An oak tree sequesters carbon. It produces oxygen. It softens our harsh landscape. It feeds squirrels. A bunch of oak in a grove around a house can substantially reduce heating fuel use.

And, for good measure: According to the US Forestry Service, bur oak trees support 534 butterfly and moth species, more than any other native prairie plant!

While you're at it, plant ten.

A NOBLE
WAY TO
NURTURE
GOOD BUGS
IN THE
NORTH

AMUR MAPLE
Autumn Orange for the Prairie

The prairie's alkaline soils usually prevent orange fall colors. The Amur maple can be an exception, sometimes turning orange, other times a deep red, with mottlings of yellow.

In Minnesota, Amur maple have been declared a noxious weed because their seed spreads into wooded areas, altering the habitat. Some people will object to planting them.

On the northern prairie, however, Amur simply do not spread like they do further east. It is possible that the alkaline soils are just hostile enough to keep the tree in check. Plant Amur maple without guilt.

An Amur maple shows its autumn colors along US Highway 59 near Elizabeth, MN.

AMERICAN
BITTERSWEET

The bittersweet is a native vine known for its brilliant orange fruit which dries on the vine and can be used in winter arrangements. However, growing bittersweet domestically has always been a crap shoot, as you needed both a male and female plant for pollination, and it is impossible to tell them apart at the time of purchase.

The recently-introduced Autumn Revolution™ bittersweet has what are called "perfect" flowers—that is, the plant contains both male and female characteristics. This advance in breeding means one can purchase only one plant and be assured it will bear fruit.

RED
GERANIUMS

A simple planter at Bergeson Nursery, left, shows how the red geranium blooms can be set off by white bacopa. Alyssum or white petunias also work. Geraniums come in a wide variety of colors, but the bright reds stand out most.

Just a few red geraniums in a pot or two provide a boost of color to the front of a home. No flower is so explosive in its ability to brighten a scene otherwise dominated by concrete, brick and iron.

The above picture was taken in Lisbon, ND. I did knock to ask permission, but only the cat was home.

Geraniums prefer to grow in a pot, as they like their roots well-drained and warm. Unlike the trailing petunias, geraniums won't pout much if left to dry out a couple of times per summer.

A SPRINKLE OF WHITE
Makes Colors Come Alive

These white ageratum planted beneath hardy roses set off the rose blooms, and keep the scene complete when the roses bloom more sparsely in late summer.

This bed of impatiens in deep shade wouldn't be as vivid without a smattering of white to set off the darker shades.

An all-white bed, such as this whimsical arrangement at Rainbow Gardens in Mayville, ND, has a monochromatic charm.

RED SPLENDOR

After introducing the Red Splendor flowering crabapple to the nursery trade in 1948, the author's grandfather Melvin Bergeson promoted its planting along the main streets of dozens of prairie towns, including Shelly, MN, pictured here.

A TREE FOR WINTER FUN

The Red Splendor Flowering Crab was named, not for its pink spring bloom, but due to its bright red "persistent" fruit, the term for berries which hang on all winter.

Along the main streets of many small Red River Valley towns, the Red Splendor brightens the dull November and December scenery, before the berries dull themselves. They remain on the tree as a feast for any number of bird species, especially grouse and cedar waxwings.

Berries that remain on the tree into April often ferment, which can lead to staggering robins.

Planters liven the downtown streets of Yankton, SD.

MUNICIPAL PLANTERS

The introduction of the trailing petunias in the 1990s spawned a boom in municipal hanging baskets and planters. Cities competed to outdo each other in beautifying their main streets.

But the work!

It soon became apparent that for a city to do it right, they need a water truck, and somebody to water almost daily.

Cities have moved towards bigger baskets—the little ones get beat up, dry out, and are finished by July 4.

Now, several prairie towns are adding very large planters placed on the sidewalk. Such planters need less water, are easy to weed and maintain.

Thomas is one of several volunteers who keep tiny Kennedy, MN's many planters flourishing.

TAMARACK AND LARCH
A Novelty
On the Prairie

Larch and tamarack (*Larix*) are gaining a niche on the northern prairie, unique because they are a *deciduous conifer*—that is, they drop their needles each fall.

Telling apart the larch from the tamarack is difficult. No need to fret. If you can get ahold of small seedlings of either tree through a soil conservation service or mail order catalog, pick up a few and plant them. They grow very fast as young trees, and although the seedlings don't always take, those that do are there for the long haul.

Larch and tamarack aren't neat in appearance, nor do they have winter color, since their needles drop. But the few mature trees on the prairie are landmarks, and draw attention when their needles turn egg-yolk yellow in late fall.

This aged specimen of Larix graces McKennan Park in Sioux Falls, SD.

These imported Siberean larch (Larix siberica) at Big Sioux Nursery north of Watertown, SD, survived a drought while a row of native tamarack, once in the foreground, died. Planting either larch or tamarack seedlings is a low-cost gamble with potential for big rewards.

A stand of native tamarack (Larix laricina) at Tamarac National Wildlife Refuge near Detroit Lakes, MN.

This farmstead entrance east of Kindred, ND is lined with mature, planted bur oak. What a rarity! Somebody about eighty years back had vision and patience. Spread a good distance apart and growing in grass, these oak are in a situation which mirrors the oak savannah landscape that dominated the northern prairie for thousands of years. These bur oak will likely last generations.

BUR OAK
The Elder Statesman
of Prairie Trees

No other tree is more deserving of a place in every northern prairie yard than the noble, native bur oak (*Quercus macrocarpa*). A stalwart for millennia, well-spaced oak once graced the prairie in an arrangement now labeled *oak savannah*.

Human activity, particularly after white settlement, upset that natural arrangement. Bur oak had relied on prairie fires to eliminate more vigorous competitor trees. Intensive agriculture did away with prairie fires for good.

Although we still have substantial oak forests along rivers, actual oak savannah acres have dwindled from the millions to the several hundreds.

The problem with our present bur oak forests...

Prairie fires once killed the competitors to oak. Without the fires, most native bur oak now live in unnaturally thick forests, crowded by siblings of their own species, and encroached upon by more vigorous trees such as ash and quaking aspen.

The tight quarters cause the oak's lower branches to die, then rot. The rot spreads to the trunk. In bur oak woods growing in thick stands, a single tree usually lasts only 110 to 120 years before dying from the rot itself, or falling over in a storm due to the rot's damage to the trunk's structure.

Meanwhile, bur oak spaced in the ancient manner can live up to 300 years.

The truly long-lived bur oak is free of competition, and a healthy distance from the next bur oak, just as the millions of bur oak on the prairie were for thousands of years.

Luckily, the northern prairie yard is an ideal place for a bur oak to establish and last for centuries, with inadvertent human assistance. In lieu of fires, humans help the oak by surrounding them with grass, which is mowed, stifling competitor trees.

Raising oak from acorns is worthwhile and possible, if a bit difficult. Acorns can be planted four-to-six inches deep in tilled soil. After setting a tap root, they will emerge next season, already well-anchored.

Sadly, squirrels are fond of digging up planted acorns, even when thousands of the unplanted nuts are laying on the ground in plain view. Laying mesh over the top of the new planting helps, but squirrels will often find a way to get around that, too. There's something about a planted acorn that triggers the squirrel's legendary determination.

Planting acorns in a protected and tended garden space and moving the little seedlings later can work, but is easier said than done. The bur oak sends down a tap root which exceeds the height of the young tree, and moving a three-foot seedling in a manner which preserves that root requires machinery!

Nurseries have developed ways to start oak from acorns. Some start the acorns growing on a screen in dark, moist conditions, but out of the soil. After the acorn sends a little white root through the screen, the acorn is removed, which snaps off the tip of the root. When planted in the ground, an acorn with its tap root thus nipped will send out roots in a contained area, which makes the seedling tree easier to dig for sale a couple of years later.

You gain a few years and save yourself a lot of frustration by letting the big nurseries get the oak through toddlerhood. That's just what nurseries do!

Purchase small trees about three or four feet in height. They are on the market, usually through soil conservation services, but not always. One hopes that will change as we seek large numbers of trees to replace the green ash.

Slightly larger but more costly nursery-grown bur oak also work well. Stick to trees under six feet tall, as bur oak transplanted any larger lack the root to put on much growth in the first few years at a new location. You are better off planting a small tree with root in proper proportion to the top than watching a larger oak struggle to establish root and eventually give up the attempt.

HELPING
BUR OAK INTO
ADULTHOOD

To start new oak, we must give the young trees a few years of care. Most importantly, we must protect juvenile oak from deer, who stunt or kill the tree by nipping the buds and stripping the foliage.

The only certain way to keep the deer at bay is a heavy wire cage—or a vigilant outside dog that doesn't take vacations.

We also must protect the trunk of young oak against the usual threats: Rodents, rabbits, weed trimmers and excess mulch. This means employing those ugly white tubes.

Happily, the bur oak develops the protective corky bark earlier than other trees, at which point trunk protection is no longer needed.

Those who plant a young oak will be pleasantly surprised by the speed of the young tree's growth, and satisfied with the tree's dignified appearance in its first decade.

After ten years, a bur oak will survive on its own more dependably than most children do after eighteen years.

Leave A Legacy for 100s of Years

Planting and establishing a new bur oak is uniquely satisfying, as the planter has likely improved our landscape for generations, and in a way which returns a small portion of the prairie to its ancient state.

The gnarled branches of this mature bur oak show their stolid character after their leaves drop in the fall. A jack-o-lantern at the base of this tree would complete the picture.

OTHER OAK
And Why We Don't Need Them

Common bur oak raised from acorns are part of the white oak *species*. They promise nothing more than solid performance and predictable results. For the urban yard designer, that is quite boring.

So, many new *cultivars* of white oak have entered the market with more on the way. Most were selected or bred for urban situations and feature a tighter shape, or perhaps slightly faster growth. Such oak hybrids often incorporate English oak, or other oak families in their genetics.

As long as they are designated as Zone 3 hardy, such named varieties of oak are fine to try. But for the average northern prairie dweller, the named and grafted *cultivars* of oak are less wise (and more expensive) to plant than the plain old *species* raised from acorns harvested in the area.

This oak hybrid at McCrory Gardens was bred for its columnar shape. Such shapes are in high demand in urban areas, but are best regarded as a mere novelty for the prairie planter.

RED OAK AND PIN OAK

Many nurseries offer red oak (Quercus rubra), and pin oak (Quercus palustris), valued for their bright red fall color and dignified, almost formal shape. Their leaves feature lobes which come to a sharp point and often hang on throughout the winter, turning from red to a dull bronze.

A handful of pin and red oak show up native on the eastern fringe of the northern prairie, at a rate of about one for every few thousand bur oak. They make a splash in the fall, as you can see in the picture above.

Red oak and pin oak are more prevalent in the wild east and south of the northern prairie, making for spectacular red fall color displays in the hills down by Red Wing, MN. The displays make some people want to bring the varieties north and west.

See if you can find the lone native red oak amidst the quaking aspen in this scene a half-mile from the author's home.

But unlike bur oak, which thrive in a broad range of soil conditions, the red and pin oak do not like alkaline soils and frequently show signs of iron chlorosis when planted on the prairie.

Furthermore, the red and pin oak are afflicted with oak wilt, a pernicious disease which exists in the forests of southeastern Minnesota, but which has not yet advanced to the prairies to the northwest. Bur oak can be afflicted with oak wilt, but the disease seems to need red and pin oak to truly spread.

Introducing large numbers of red and pin oak to the northern prairie might be as unwise as it is unlikely to succeed.

Better for those of us on the northern prairie to insist upon the plain old bur oak, a tree that is truly ours, and which has served the prairie well for thousands of years. Let us replenish its numbers.

SPRUCE
The Northern Prairie's
Favorite Tree Import

This spruce in central SD is afflicted with disease and should be pulled out. It is in a well-protected part of town, surrounded by many buildings, and likely has suffered from lack of air movement.

Although not native to the northern prairie, Black Hills and Colorado spruce were amongst the first trees planted by the settlers. Peddlers on horseback made sure nearly every farmstead had a few spruce. Some of those peddlers' wares still stand.

In windbreaks and shelter belts, spruce have provided winter color and wind protection to countless farmsteads. In town, spruce on the corners of a lot make things cozy all year, but especially at Christmas.

In the past fifteen years, however, fungal disease has caused many spruce to decline, causing great consternation. Some go so far as to recommend not planting any more Colorado spruce, as they are more susceptible to disease than the Black Hills.

The city park in pretty Bowdle, SD is atop a hill, with plenty of wind. I suspect that is why every one of the park's many spruce, including this beautiful Colorado Blue, are free of disease.

HOPE FOR
SPRUCE

Traveling the region makes me optimistic about the future of spruce on the northern prairie, even if the disease persists at present rates.

There are so many miles of beautiful spruce plantings which remain! Yes, disease has knocked holes in some spruce windbreaks. It is also killing some spruce in town. But if planted in the proper location, and cared for wisely, both Black Hills and Colorado spruce will be with us for a long time.

The spruce diseases are fundamentally different than the emerald ash borer, which attacks like a slow-moving and unstoppable bulldozer. Diseases on spruce require specific conditions to take off, and are likely to ebb and flow with each season.

As the more vulnerable spruce—those planted tightly, those in wet areas—die off, the remaining spruce have a good chance to remain healthy.

As our knowledge of what must be done to prevent spruce disease expands and is distributed, the disease will likely decrease.

Against all odds, this beautiful Colorado blue spruce has attained perfection in the Split Rock Park in Garretson, SD: right near a body of water, in tight, wooded quarters—and in a low, damp spot at the base of the railroad grade, surrounded by sod!

The three fungal diseases which afflict spruce send their airborne spores everywhere. We likely breathe them daily. But for the spores to settle on a tree and do their dirty work, conditions must be just right.

Thankfully, humans can create conditions for spruce which can substantially reduce the risk of disease.

Here is how to raise spruce! This farmstead near Hallock is surrounded with many dozen spruce, all kept perfectly clean. The result? No disease.

This spruce in a city park in eastern South Dakota should be yanked. It was moved when too large, and struggles to grow in sod. It will not improve, nor will any spruce tree which looks like this.

Generally, spruce disease is worse in the eastern part of the northern prairie and lessens as you travel west and the humidity lowers.

Yet, I saw so many exceptions to this rule, I am not sure it should continue to be a rule. Some of the nicest spruce possible, both Black Hills and Colorado, grow in the relatively damp corridor between I-29 and the Minnesota-South Dakota border.

Out west, meanwhile, there are pockets of higher humidity where the disease manifests. Spruce do very well in Bismarck, but pretty Washburn, only 40 miles north, has slightly higher average humidity. Its spruce are suffering.

SPRUCE DISEASE PREVENTION BASICS

1) Although planting thick rows of spruce was a great strategy to stop the prairie winds, the practice is now causing problems. Spruce planted closely enough so their branches intermingle are highly likely to get disease. Lack of air movement allows the spores to reproduce by the billion during wet days in June. Soil conservation services are now recommending that spruce be planted 15-25 feet apart.

2) Spruce with tall grass and weeds growing up into the lower branches, as well as in the immediate vicinity of the tree, are *almost certain* to get fungal disease. Grass and weeds hinder air movement and harbor the disease. Keeping the soil clean out to the tips of the branches for the first ten to fifteen years after planting is crucial.

3) Spruce with mowed sod right up to their trunks struggle as well, and for more reasons than disease. Young spruce simply do not put on new growth when forced to compete with sod. Keep the soil out to the tips of the branches lightly tilled, or kill the grass and weeds with herbicide. Tilled soil is better than heavy mulching, or use of fabric, which seems to weaken the tree. I have never yet seen a row of spruce that is kept completely clean of grass and weeds—including between the rows—afflicted with the fungal diseases.

LET'S KEEP PLANTING SPRUCE

As long as we are willing to give spruce plenty of space and keep them free of weeds and grass, we can and should continue to plant them all across the northern prairie.

I will go further, and differ with many experts: there are so many healthy Colorado spruce on the northern prairie that we need not eliminate the pretty species from consideration.

No non-native tree has contributed more to the prairie landscape over the past one hundred years than spruce. There is no reason why that tradition cannot continue.

Should I Spray My Spruce With Fungicide?

Spruce diseases require specific atmospheric conditions, and so do the fungicides which kill them. It is very difficult to get the timing right. Even professional applicators specifically trained in spruce diseases acknowledge that it is difficult for them.

In addition, spruce which already show the disease are not likely to show much improvement even with an aggressive spray program. Spruce that already look bad should simply be pulled out.

With all the knowledge we have about how to prevent spruce disease, that may be all that is needed.

Spraying fungicide on spruce which are full of weeds, or planted too tightly, is a little like smoking two packs of cigarettes and day and expecting heart pills to take care of whatever problems might arise.

Even in the best conditions, old spruce lose their lower branches and become a bit sparse.

STARTING SPRUCE

The soil conservation services usually stock small spruce seedlings. They have bare root seedlings in spring, and sometimes small potted spruce during the summer.

Planting bare root is preferable, assuming you get them in the ground right after purchase. Make sure to plant bare root spruce seedlings deeply, with the soil touching the lower needles. Deeper planting protects the seedling from dehydration (desiccation) during hot late-spring winds the first season.

They don't have to be in rows! These two spruce in the middle of a field show one farmer's willingness to put up with some hassle to add character to the prairie landscape.

To start larger spruce, the best bet is to find field-dug spruce from area wholesale nurseries such as Lundeby Evergreens in Tolna, ND. Lundeby's plops their beautiful trees in bushel baskets as soon as spring hits.

Do not allow the dirt ball to fall apart while planting. Field-dug spruce come in bushel baskets which go in the ground at planting and rot quickly. (For more information on starting spruce, see *Successful Gardening on the Northern Prairie.*)

A healthy row of established, well-spaced spruce south of Thief River Falls, MN, cuts a dramatic profile during a winter sunset.

Potted spruce purchased at the box stores are generally root-bound. They dry out quickly in the ground, and many perish the first winter. In addition to being root-bound, their foliage is soft due to excess fertilization. They are often quite cheap, but the percentage of success is low.

Spruce up to six feet can be safely moved in with a tree spade. Spruce trees larger than eight feet are a poor bet no matter how they are moved.

LILAC

As I drove the back highways in eastern North Dakota in June of 2019, I was treated to mile after mile of lilac blooming in the mature windbreaks planted during the 1940s and 1950s. The old lilac hedges of North Dakota showed a variety of color, from the typical lavender, to pink, to dark pink, to white.

In every small town, mounds of old lilac bloomed in a festival of nostalgia.

Then, just as the bloom reached its peak, one day of fifty-mile-per-hour winds and ninety-degree heat turned the blooms brown. Our week of fun ended.

Some people long for recurring lilac bloom. In fact, a dwarf lilac has been bred which re-blooms in August.

But the charm of the lilac remains its ability to give us one week of concentrated, transcendent beauty.

Common lilac shelter belt planting near Mahnomen, MN.

A classic multi-colored grouping of lilac in their glory
near the Assemblies of God church in Finley, ND.

What if lilac were to bloom all summer? We would get sick of them in a hurry. The scent would become annoying to some, and cause allergies in others.

We value things in direct proportion to their rarity.

To enjoy lilac bloom to the maximum, take time during the busy time of late spring to amble out to the old windbreak and cut a bouquet. Cut several! Put them around the house.

When in one week the bouquets fade, you'll wistfully be done with them, just as most of us are ready to put the Christmas decorations away come New Year's Day.

A Pocahontas lilac near St. John's Lutheran Church in rural Fertile, MN. Pocahontas is a hybrid which blooms on younger shrubs and grows more vigorously than the species common lilac.

A white common lilac blooms its heart out in a handsome arrangement found in southeastern Finley, ND.

Almost without fail, lilac are worry-free and dependable. During their bloom, they produce a week of magic similar to Christmas.

On the northern prairie, the more lilac the merrier.

KOREAN LILAC

The Korean lilac, often labeled "dwarf," blooms heavily with small, fragrant blossoms just after the common lilac blooms fade. Used heavily in landscapes, the shrub seldom stays as dwarf as advertised, necessitating heavy trimming to keep it under five or six feet. Such trimming results in a formal, aggressively round look. Planted in a short row out in the yard, the Dwarf Korean can be allowed to grow more naturally.

CANADIAN LILAC
Extend the Lilac Bloom Season

The lilac season can be extended by adding Prestonian hybrids, otherwise known as Canadian lilacs, to our plantings. The "Miss Canada," pictured here, is a spectacular pink, completely hardy, and blooms about 10 days later than the common lilac. Canadian lilacs survive alkaline soils better than the common lilac, which can struggle in low spots on the prairie. For longer hedges, the Villosa lilac, a seed-grown Canadian lilac, is often available in small starters through the soil conversation services. Canadian lilacs do not send out suckers like the common lilac.

Mildew!

In a moist season such as 2019, lilac leaves can become white with powdery mildew in mid-summer and cause some panic. The mildew problem is cosmetic, and varies from season to season. Nothing need be done, for by the time the mildew is noticed, it has already done its worst.

MISS KIM
A Superior Dwarf Lilac

A Miss Kim Dwarf Lilac thrives at a residence in Crookston, MN.

T he bloom and foliage of the "Miss Kim" dwarf lilac are more striking than the Dwarf Korean, but Miss Kim are seldom planted, for unknown reasons. The Miss Kim's large, heavily-scented blooms are held upright. Its leaves are larger than the Dwarf Korean's, and are cupped upward in an oriental manner. In addition, the Miss Kim has striking fall leaf color, ranging from a deep purple to a bright yellow.

The hydrangea paniculata "Vanilla Strawberry" is a highly popular pink. Its blooms are so huge that they droop on younger plants, a problem which decreases over time as the shrub gains strength.

HYDRANGEA
Plant More, But of the Right Kinds

On my travels across the northern prairie, no plant was more glaringly absent in the landscape than hydrangea, in all its wonderful forms.

Forgiving, easy to grow, easy to maintain, one grouping of hydrangea in a single yard can become the focal point of an entire city block. Hydrangea put on a show.

Why are hydrangea not planted more often? Well, they have been, but people have been buying the wrong ones!

DON'T
GET THE
BLUES

Most of the hydrangea hype goes to new varieties with blue and lavender blooms. The pictures, and indeed the plants sold in pots at the box stores, create the impression that we can grow the spectacular hydrangeas you'd see in Seattle, or other warmer climes with acid soil.

Indeed, some of these highly-touted hydrangea work reasonably well in the Twin Cities and Chicago, markets which determine what varieties are shipped out to the box stores in Bismarck and Aberdeen.

So, prairie people buy the hype and buy the plant, only to have it struggle, turn yellow, produce few blooms, and finally die.

And the prairie planter gets disillusioned with anything called hydrangea.

Hydrangea aborescens is dramatic wherever it is planted, and if kept well-watered, can endure two-thirds of a day of sunshine, as it does here in Bergeson Gardens.

LET'S LEARN A LITTLE LATIN

Sometimes, learning a little Latin can be a big help. It is the best way to sort through all of the hydrangea varieties on the market. The Latin name should be on the label.

Hydrangea *aborescens* and hydrangea *paniculata* work on the northern prairie. Hydrangea *macrophylla* do poorly, but get all the hype, and create false hope.

Hydrangea *arborescens* thrive in shade, and can take up to half-a-day of sun. Their leaves are large, soft and a bit limp, similar to the leaves of a basswood. The canes can be cut to the ground each spring and the plant will bloom on the new growth.

Hydrangea *paniculata* thrive in sun, but can withstand up to half-a-day of shade. Their leaves are stiff, with raised veins, and crack easily when bent. The shrub *cannot* be cut back to the ground each year, as they will not bloom.

Thankfully, hydrangea *paniculata* come in a wide variety of eventual heights. To avoid the need for harsh trimming, simply choose a variety which won't get too big for your spot.

If you are eager to plant hydrangea next spring, take some time this winter to learn these Latin words!

The blooms on the Hydrangea paniculata, such as this "Limelight," tend to be conical rather than globe-shaped, as are the hydrangea arborescens flowers.

101

Hydrangea are ideal for institutional buildings. They are tough, require little care, and are bold enough in appearance to soften the most domineering brick and concrete monoliths.

(Above) A hydrangea paniculata variety doing well in a planter outside a Ramsey County government building in downtown St. Paul, a truly hostile setting for living things.

(Left) A splash of hydrangea arborescens does wonders for the drab concrete entrance to the administration building of the University of South Dakota in Vermillion.

A mass of hydrangea has done well for decades on the north side of the Duane Knutson Community Center in Fertile, MN.

THOSE THAT WORK...

Meanwhile, new hydrangea that *do* work for our area are being introduced each year! By choosing the right varieties, which can most easily be found at locally owned nurseries, one can grow hydrangea in shade or sun, hydrangea that are tall or short, white or pink, with blooms that are tight and full, or loose and elegant.

There are dozens, with more coming out each year.

Hydrangea paniculata "Quickfire" features blooms that start white, then turn pink and eventually mauve.

A Quickfire hydrangea paniculata at the Halstad Living Center in Halstad, MN, doing very well in Halstad's heavy, alkaline soil.

An Invicibelle ® Hydrangea growing in Clark, SD. The Invicibelle is a true pioneer: a variety of the shade-loving hydrangea that blooms pink!

103

The tree-form hydrangea paniculata are a shrub grafted onto a trunk called a "standard." The result is novel, but expensive, and the single trunk is more vulnerable to winter injury than a hydrangea grown like it is meant to be grown: as a shrub.

GIVE YOUR HYDRANGEA A BOOST

The hydrangea varieties we grow on the prairie are remarkably forgiving, and can do acceptably well in our existing soil. But it is well worth the effort to amend the soil and fertilize, for they will do so much better!

First, hydrangea benefit from a complete, or nearly complete, replacement of the existing soil with northern sedge peat. Put the new plant in a hole the size of a five-gallon pail, and replace the soil with pure peat. The addition of any amount of peat will help.

Second, hydrangea simply explode in response to applications of our favorite prairie fertilizer, ammonium sulphate. Ammonium sulphate accomplishes the same task as the expensive acid fertilizers in colorful boxes, at less than one-tenth the cost.

And yes, when it gets dry, hydrangea need water.

There is no reason every town on the northern prairie shouldn't plant lots of hydrangea!

TATARIAN
MAPLE

The Hot Wings® Tatarian maple is a small, shapely tree which produces bright red "samaras," otherwise known as "helicopters," that make a striking display for the last half of summer. Hot Wings is tolerant of alkaline soils, and is being used on boulevards in Bismarck, ND, where overhead wires require a shorter tree.

Quaking Aspen in Gettysburg, SD

108

QUAKING ASPEN

On the eastern fringes of the northern prairie, wild quaking aspen grow in fast-expanding colonies which can encroach on yards and fields.

The temptation is to dismiss quaking aspen as a weed. Indeed, few people in the east third of the northern prairie plant quaking aspen in their yards. Seems there are enough already.

As you move west, the frequency of rogue mass forestations of the tree diminishes. Lo and behold, quaking aspen begin to appear in people's yards. By the time you reach Bismarck, it is a staple of the domestic landscape.

We shouldn't forget the tree's delights, most prominently, the rustling leaves, which twinkle in slightest breeze. The tree's latin name, *Populus tremuloides,* alludes to the visual and musical pleasures quaking aspen produce. Their leaves *tremble,* and the sounds they produce are *tremulous.*

When planted as a specimen, the tree can be dignified and svelte, with a greenish-white bark that adds an artistic touch to winter.

SHOULD I TEST
MY PRAIRIE SOIL?

By all means. Here's how:

Before planting a garden, shrub or tree, add sedge peat.
All northern prairie soils can use the organic matter
peat provides.

Second, after planting, apply ammonium sulphate
fertilizer regularly. All prairie soils and the plants
planted in them benefit from the boost of nitrogen and
the lowering of pH that ammonium sulphate provides.

Water deeply as needed.

Watch the plants grow. The probability that
they will do well is close to one-hundred
percent.

On the odd chance that some nutritional deficiency still
exists, the plant will tell you what is missing by
exhibiting symptoms that an expert can analyze.

If you live in the parts of the prairie where salts and
alkalinity are completely out of hand, you probably
know it without testing. Consult your county's soil and
water district to find out which trees cope the best.

There you have it: soil test completed. For free!

AN ASPIRING SPIRE?

The striking column in this photo is a Taylor juniper, shown here thriving into maturity in the Zone 3 environs at the NDSU Horticultural Experiment Station near Absaraka, ND. Discovered in Nebraska and rated for Zone 5, the Taylor Juniper with its striking shape, is slowly moving north. If it continues to succeed, Taylor juniper will provide a dramatic additon to the northern prairie's landscape.

THE PRAIRIE PLANTER'S PLIGHT

Once convinced of the merit of a plant for the prairie, such as a bur oak, or a hybrid cottonwood—or a gardening product, such as ammonium sulphate or sedge peat, the question arises: Where can I get it?

The answer is always the same: It is out there, but you have to look around.

Every little local nursery stocks different plants. It is worth the drive, as long as you stay within your climate zone, or go north.

If you know the exact Latin name of the plant you seek, it doesn't matter if the nursery that stocks it is out of the area.

Consult with other gardeners and share starters.

See what your county's soil conservation district has to offer.

The Globe Caragana is an ideal low-maintenance shrub for cemeteries and for home plantings. It could be the prairie's answer to boxwood, thriving in drought and alkaline soils. Here planted at the cemetery in Ada, MN, this globe caragana will stay compact for decades with little or no trimming. But you have to dig a little to find one!

Somebody dropped off seed for this striking hollyhock at the nursery. Passing around unusual and hard-to-find plants is a time-honored gardening practice!

Our situation on the northern prairie is unique. We are faced with alkaline soils. Most of the nation's population lives on acid soils. In addition, we are colder than the rest of the country. By a lot.

What makes it worse is there aren't enough people in our situation for the national market to pay attention to our needs. At the very most, there are 2.5 million northern prairie residents, less than one percent of our country's population.

Filling our singular horticultural needs takes pluck and determination.

Although it blooms at a time (early June) when we could use the color, the gas plant (Dictamnus) is rare on the mass market. If you can find one, buy it. Once established, they last forever. And when the pods dry in late July, you can light a match near them and they will go "poof!"

SOLUTIONS UNDER OUR NOSE

Sometimes, the solution to finding what we need is simple. The best fertilizer for the northern prairie yard is ammonium sulphate. Ammonium sulphate is superior to any fertilizer in colorful packages, and more appropriate for our soils than anything advertised nationally.

Most small farm-town fertilizer plants have ammonium sulphate for pennies per pound.

Yet even with ammonium sulphate, there is disbelief that something could be so simple.

A lady I spoke with in western North Dakota reported that her husband wouldn't let her go to the fertilizer plant to get ammonium sulphate because they would think she was nuts.

So, she ordered some on Amazon—and paid, with shipping, $70 for a 10-pound bag!

It was worth it. Her trees and shrubs perked up dramatically.

Her husband still won't let her go to the fertilizer plant to get ammonium sulphate—he goes there himself!

A young Ohio Buckeye in Hillsboro, ND. Ohio Buckeye are an ideal moderate-sized tree for northern prairie yards, but can be difficult to find. Luckily, it is easy to start one from an Ohio Buckeye nut!

A SECRET APPLE

Introduced by the University of Minnesota in 1949, the Chestnut apple has a devoted, if small, following, but has never really taken off. Yet, almost everybody who tastes one is hooked.

The apple's top-notch flavor, pear-like aftertaste, beautiful appearance and Zone 3 hardiness make it perfect for the northern prairie.

However, the Chestnut has a liability: its fruit is too small to be marketed. What's worse, the fact that its fruits are sometimes less than two inches across has led it to be carelessly tossed in the category of "crab" rather than "apple." That unfortunate and unfair designation, which has nothing to do with the superb quality of the Chestnut's fruit, has consigned the apple to obscurity.

"One of the best kept secrets in Minnesota," said an old nurseryman of the Chestnut, and he is right.

With heirloom apples coming into fashion, the Chestnut might be on its way out of hiding. But these things happen slowly. Even though Chestnut has made its way to the very top of South Dakota State extension's list of recommended fruits, I spoke to crowds of over 50 gardeners in some South Dakota towns where *not one person* had even heard of it!

No wonder it is tough to get ahold of one! You'll never find a Chestnut at the box stores, that much is certain.

A SOLUTION...

The Chestnut apple is available on the wholesale market. The trick is to get a local nursery to buy some, and here is how you get that to happen:

Nurseries order apple trees by the bundles of five or ten. Nursery owners are not keen to buy a whole bundle of ten to fill an order of one tree for one person of a tree nobody's ever heard of. They're likely to have nine left at the end of the season. Turn that trick too many times and you're out of business.

To overcome the nurseryman's hesitance, find some friends. Band together and promise to purchase all ten trees of the type you want. Put down a down payment. Do this in March, when every nurseryman feels, and likely is, nearly broke. In fact, you should be able to get a reduced price.

So many of the trees and plants that are ideal for the northern prairie, such as the Chestnut, and the plain old bur oak, and the plain old sugar maple, get no attention in the bigger markets. Wholesalers sometimes stock them, but in small numbers. They are a tough sell.

But if we band together in the manner of the co-operative movements of 100 years ago, or even just as a band of neighbors, we can overcome. And if enough of us do this for enough years in a row, wholesale nurseries will respond by increasing supply.

A hardier tree than the Honeycrisp, the Zestar apple, also introduced by the University of Minnesota, has produced some of the largest apples seen on the northern prairie in a good year.

Originating from Manitoba, the Goodland apple is Zone 3 hardy and bears on young trees despite its vigorous growth habit. Recent experience suggests that prairie apple trees benefit from vigor, even if it means using a ladder to pick the apples.

APPLE TREES
Standard or Dwarf?

For the past few decades, dwarf apples trees have been popular. Smaller trees, the argument goes, don't take up so much space, keep their apples lower for easier picking, and actually can bear sooner in their lifetime.

All apple trees are grafted, but dwarf apple trees are grafted onto a special root which stunts the top.

The problem? The dwarfing root stock is not as hardy as the traditional "standard" root stock, which is taken from a seedling of the very hardy Dolgo Crab, or equally tough Siberian Crab. During a winter when there is little snow cover, the dwarf root stocks can freeze, killing the entire tree.

In addition, by sapping the tree of its vigor, the dwarfing rootstock may produce a tree which is less able to withstand the adversity dealt out by the northern prairie.

Although it is true that an apple tree which is too vigorous can refuse to bloom and bear, it is equally true that a certain amount of vigor is needed to recover from winter injuries and out-run summer pests.

While dwarf apple trees will likely continue to be popular in urban areas, those of us in the wide open spaces of the northern prairie are best served by purchasing apple trees that are as strong as possible.

In other words, it is best to stick to the old-time "standard" root stocks, even if it means that the tree gets large. A tree that grows large is a healthy tree, and we humans can always purchase one of those long apple-picking poles if we simply must get at all those apples out of our reach.

SOIL
CONSERVATION
DISTRICTS

After I announced a tour of South Dakota cities, a lady from the Madison Area Arts Council wrote and offered to host my talk in their Arts Center.

A nice crowd of about 20 showed up, and included some folks from the Lake County Soil Conservation District, which had generously promoted my talk on social media.

I brought up the Chestnut Apple. Nobody had heard of it. "Hmm," said one of the soil conservation folks, "maybe we should stock it."

The young man had no idea the land mine he had tripped into.

The 3,000 soil and water conservation districts in this country were founded by state law to help preserve our natural amenities through many methods, one of which is the planting of trees. Believing that tree planting is a public good, the decision was made at both state and federal levels in the 1930s and 1940s to subsidize their planting. Some states, including North and South Dakota, as well as Minnesota, even founded state-owned nurseries to supply the trees.

My grandfather, a proponent of the free market as well as the owner of a nursery that produced trees by the thousand, was dead set against the government flooding the market with subsidized trees. He traveled to St. Paul to testify against such socialism, or "bolshevism," as he called it during his testimony.

A windbreak of green ash north of Warren, MN

Grandpa won over one legislative committee, but ultimately, state government subsidies for tree planting won the day.

Later in life, Grandpa saw the wisdom of the soil and water conservation districts selling small trees that would otherwise be unavailable. He sold trees to the districts by the tens of thousands, and some of his best friends were the good tree-loving folks who staffed the SCD offices.

But where he drew the line was if the soil conservation districts started selling yard trees for reduced prices, thus undercutting local nurseries.

So, when the young man from the soil conservation service said, "Hmm, maybe we should stock those," about the Chestnut apple, which is yard tree, and which will never be planted in large enough numbers to stave off soil erosion, I rankled.

I wish I hadn't.

Getting the free market to respond to our tree needs on the northern prairie is often like beating a dead mule.

The urgency of getting trees planted on the northern prairie is such that we should have all hands on deck.

Of course, before stocking specimen yard trees at reduced prices, each conservation service would, I hope, evaluate the availability of those trees on the local private market.

But soil and water conservation districts have a role to play, particularly as we seek to replace the masses of green ash doomed by the emerald ash borer. And their role is larger the more remote the county.

If you want savvy advice about what trees work locally, you will get some of the best tips available from the long-time staffer at the soil conservation office who may not have a degree in horticulture, but who knows what has worked and what hasn't through years of experience. His or her advice will be, by definition, more specific to your area than the advice from a state-wide extension service, or for that matter, any book I might write.

A week or two after I visited Madison, I stopped at 10 a.m. in Ipswich, SD. It was a dark morning, heavy with imminent rain. We huddled in a downtown gazebo for protection, but people kept coming, so some got wet.

One of those who stood in the rain was a lady from the Emmons County Soil and Water Conservation District. I was honored she came, and glad she stayed!

From her I learned that the soils are so alkaline and the salts so high in Emmons County that they can grow little other than the old (and now broadly despised) Siberian Elm, and the old messy cottonwood, which she informed me can take drought and alkalinity better than the newer hybrids.

What a pleasure it was to visit with somebody with local expertise.

What a boon that every county on the northern prairie has the same.

A row of hybrid poplar west of Fertile, MN.

WORTHWHILE WILLOW

As the Flame Willow matures, it maintains a neat-shaped form with upswept branches. Melvin Bergeson, who introduced the tree, suggested cutting the Flame Willow to the ground every ten years and letting it come back with fresh, vigorous, growth that has a deeper orange color.

The Flame Willow is best grown as a shrub, with branches to the ground. It does not drop branches like the weeping willow.

Prairie Reflection® Willow, a top-notch introduction from North Dakota State University, features dark, glossy leaves on a fast-growing, yet tightly-rounded tree. Don't wrinkle your nose when you hear the word "willow!" Some of them are excellent and deserving of space in our yards.

NORTHERN CATALPA

Known for its dramatic large leaves and orchid-like bloom, the Northern Catalpa makes for a striking novelty tree in Zone 4 and 3b of the northern prairie.

Catalpa trees in the northern reaches of the region tend to grow best as large shrubs, with branches left on to the ground. Occasionally they will suffer some winter dieback. They require protection from winter winds, so do best in town.

In Zone 4, the catalpa can grow into a massive specimen worthy of planting on the boulevard.

You won't find a bloom like the catalpa's on any other northern prairie tree.

This pair of catalpas in Twin Valley, MN, grow as catalpa typically do farther north: with branches to the ground.

ECHINACEA
Native to the Prairie

Echinacea are increasing in popularity, and
breeders have responded by introducing a wide
variety of colors. Echinacea are coveted by the
entire country, but originated on the northern
prairie and grow better here than in warmer,
wetter climes. Yes, we have something to flaunt!

The striking orange center is part of the appeal of the native Echinacea purpurea.

The echinacea pictured here are a small part of the very large coneflower family, most of which exist only in the wild as what we would call yellow daisies.

Echinacea are native to the prairie, which means they can take alkaline soil and they can take it dry.

Echinacea do not respond well to heavy mulching and automatic watering systems. In regions with damp wet winters, they frequently die of rot.

An elegant white echinacea purpurea

Although frequently used in corporate landscapes as individual plants surrounded by rock, the echinacea makes the most impact in the prairie garden if planted in a natural-looking mass.

Breeders are developing echinacea which are wide-petaled, round, chubby, cute—and orange, all of which are popular, but not quite as prairie-like.

A variety of echinacea planted in a mass next to another native prairie perennial, liatrus, at McCrory Gardens in Brookings, SD.

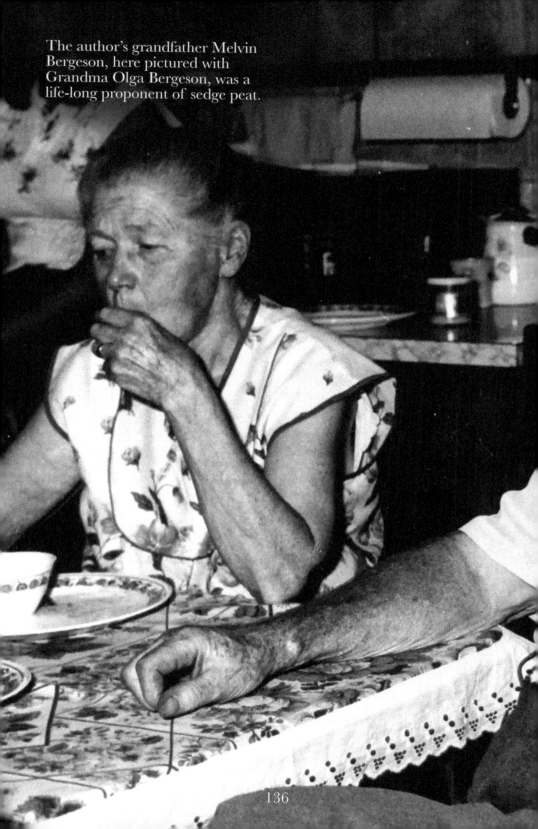

The author's grandfather Melvin Bergeson, here pictured with Grandma Olga Bergeson, was a life-long proponent of sedge peat.

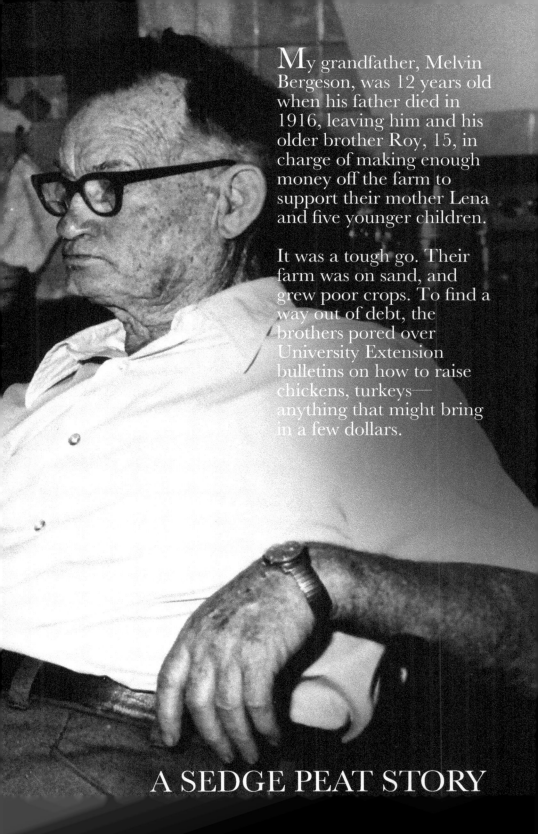

My grandfather, Melvin Bergeson, was 12 years old when his father died in 1916, leaving him and his older brother Roy, 15, in charge of making enough money off the farm to support their mother Lena and five younger children.

It was a tough go. Their farm was on sand, and grew poor crops. To find a way out of debt, the brothers pored over University Extension bulletins on how to raise chickens, turkeys—anything that might bring in a few dollars.

A SEDGE PEAT STORY

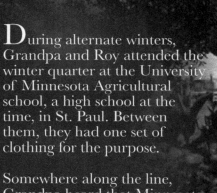

During alternate winters, Grandpa and Roy attended the winter quarter at the University of Minnesota Agricultural school, a high school at the time, in St. Paul. Between them, they had one set of clothing for the purpose.

Somewhere along the line, Grandpa heard that Minnesota sedge peat was ideal for growing strawberries. During a dry year, he found that the swamp right next to their little house in Twin Valley had peat.

Grandpa ordered strawberries by mail and planted them in the peat ground. They flourished the first year, but Mama criticized him for spending so much time tending the strawberries when he could have been out in the fields making hay, or helping with the livestock.

The next year came the first strawberry crop. It was huge. Grandpa picked the plump berries and sold them door-to-door on horseback. Times were tough, but people couldn't resist. In those few weeks, he made enough money to pay that year's payment on the farm.

Mama never complained about Grandpa's berry tending again. And Grandpa was on his way to become a nurseryman.

After working as a salesman for Gurney's Nursery in Yankton, SD, Grandpa came home ready to start a nursery. His big break came when he married Olga Johnson.

Grandma Olga owned a farm she purchased from her ailing parents for one dollar. On that land, Grandpa found peat. Lots of peat.

We don't know whether Grandpa found the peat before or after he proposed to Grandma.

Well-married, Grandpa was on his way to fulfilling his dream: owning a nursery. He started it in 1936.

The peat on Grandma's farm soon ran out, so Grandpa moved down the road to bogs owned by neighbors, exhausting one little swamp at a time.

The soil for the "logs afire" bed consists of nothing more than a few loader buckets of pure sedge peat.

Grandpa used peat in everything Bergeson Nursery grew. When they started to raise greenhouse plants in the late 1950s, Grandpa made the unorthodox decision to raise everything in pure peat. It worked.

The tradition of digging peat each year continued after Grandpa sold the business to his son (my father) Paul and his wife Glenda (my mother). Eventually Dad discovered a large peat bog only one-half mile from the nursery which served us for thirty years.

In the spring, customers came for pickup loads of peat to spread on their vegetable and flower beds. For the most successful gardeners, it was an annual ritual.

The heavy soils of the northern prairie seem to absorb the peat, and adding more each year keeps the soil in a state of easy-to-work mellowness.

The annual digging of peat—we used more than 500 cubic yards per year—was a struggle, as trucks and tractors sink down in the stuff, but loads of fun. Nothing felt as good as having a big peat pile before winter.

"Money in the bank!" Dad would say.

141

In about 2012, we found a company in East Grand Forks, MN, now known as Dakota Peat, which harvests peat in northwestern Minnesota to sell to golf courses across the United States. We tested their peat against that from our bog, and found it grew even more beautiful plants.

So, we shut down our bog, and now we just wait for the semis to arrive with our annual peat supply. It is not as much fun, but it sure saves on the machinery!

To this day, not a night goes by where I don't dream of mining a massive pile of peat.

We still use it pure in most pots, pure on the gardens, and pure in the bags we sell to our customers.

What is peat?

Peat is essentially plant matter that has decomposed slowly for hundreds of years beneath the water of a bog. Sedge peat is thus named because it consists almost entirely of cattail reeds. It is alternately called reed sedge peat, Canadian peat, or even "muck" peat.

Sedge peat is not to be confused with sphagnum peat, which is an only lightly decomposed moss. Sphagnum peat dominates the market, and has some benefits as a soil conditioner, but is frustrating to work with due to its dryness. It cannot be used pure.

Is sedge peat sustainable?

Sedge peat accumulates in cattail bogs at a rate of 6-8 inches per century, eventually accumulating to a depth of many feet.

Canada is one of the largest producers of sedge peat. So, how is their supply holding out?

According to a survey by the Canadian government, Canada has about 280 million acres of peat land.

Of those millions of acres, only 17,000 are under harvest.

As slow as sedge peat is to form, it is estimated that nature adds 70 times more peat to Canada's supply each year than humans subtract.

And remember: we're not burning the peat, we are merely moving it.

Why does peat work so well?

Northern sedge peat is an ideal growing medium. It holds moisture against the roots of plants at almost exactly the right rate. It isn't too dry, as sphagnum moss is, nor does it get easily waterlogged, like the heavy soils of the northern prairie.

Peat is usually acidic, which counteracts the alkalinity of the northern prairie soils.

The original peat swamp Melvin Bergeson used to start his nursery has long reverted to a wetland, home to a nesting pair of trumpeter swans for the past twenty years.

If peat is harvested carefully, and most commercial operations are very careful, it comes virtually weed-free. In our experience, most weeds come from our own carelessness at handling the peat while preparing it for use.

Why isn't sedge peat used everywhere?

A very good question, one I asked Grandpa many times.

His answer?

"They don't have a peat swamp."

In other words, we discovered the value of sedge peat because it was cheap and readily available out on the back forty.

Harvesting sedge peat is not easy, and the price it fetches is about the same as other, more easily obtained potting mixes. The massive lumber industry, for example, has flooded the market with potting soils made of decomposed wood products, a byproduct they could afford to give away.

Not all sedge peat is the same. As you move south, sedge peat becomes heavy, mucky, gray—and is sometimes referred to derisively as "muck" peat. In short, it is too decomposed.

In these regions, it is no wonder people turned to the lighter and locally available sphagnum peat.

Even in northern Minnesota, not all peat swamps are created equal. A very few isolated bogs are actually toxic to domestic plants.

In short, before you use peat you find yourself, you should test it—not in a lab, but in a pot in which you are growing plants.

Adding several inches of sedge peat allowed Kae Bergeson to plant these annuals up to 18 inches apart, knowing they would fill in quickly.

At Bergeson Nursery, we have been using sedge peat for over eighty years.

Nothing has been more important to our success and the success of our customers than ample doses of northern Minnesota sedge peat.

Kae Bergeson stands by her favorite flower bed from 2019, the same bed pictured in the two previous pages. The total retail cost for the plants: $156.

ASTILBE

There aren't many perennials with colorful blooms for shade, but astilbe fill the bill. Astilbe like two or three hours of direct sunshine each day, and love growing in beds raised with generous amounts of peat.

FORMALITY ON THE PRAIRIE?

This stunning row of American arbor vitae in north Fargo displays a sustainable level of formality.

The spectacular and extensive Munsinger Clemens
Gardens in St. Cloud, MN, is a great stop for
prairie dwellers headed to a Twins game in
Minneapolis.

At Munsinger Clemens, one can see how the
original formal design, clearly of European origins,
is being softened and adjusted to account for
prairie climate reality. Annuals are used, but more
to add color and occasional whimsy than to
produce geometric shapes.

FORMAL GARDENS

The northern prairie's climate makes long-term formal gardening difficult. People who try to create a tight maze out of boxwood hedge plants will be frustrated by winter dieback and death.

Perennial plants, meanwhile, particularly natives, just don't behave in geometric ways.

The northern prairie formal garden must rely heavily on annuals, emphasizing varieties which can be counted on to conform to a rigid design.

Travel Europe and you will likely tour palaces, churches and government buildings surrounded by tightly-disciplined hedges, flowers planted in geometric patterns, and trees trimmed to be square, oval or some other whimsical shape.

The moderate winter temperatures and ample summer sunlight of northern Europe support such formality, which has deep historic roots.

The opulent Palace of Versailles, built by King Louis XIV of France, sits on hundreds of acres of formal plantings. During the French monarchy's glory years, parties at the palace would start with drinks in a massive formal flower garden. After the party moved inside, workers entirely replaced the annual flowers with new colors and designs in preparation for the guests' departure that same evening!

All of which emphasizes the purpose of formal gardens: to impress, intimidate and control. They are beautiful to view, but one can't escape the underlying message: The king is so powerful, even nature must bend to his will!

When left untended, formal plantings quickly go to seed. Their decline is an early indication that the institutions whose grounds they adorn are running low on cash.

A stately planter at Munsinger Clemens garden in St. Cloud, MN, an old-fashioned formal garden with prairie touches. Red salvia and red verbena are combined with silver dichondra and golden moneywort vines.

157

McCrory Gardens in Brookings, SD, is moving towards an emphasis on less formal plants of native origin.

FOR PRAIRIE FORMALITY, USE ANNUALS

Annual flowers aren't subject to winter's destructive whims. The garden designer is liberated to try different schemes each season.

This layer cake flower bed features, from center to perimeter:

Limelight Hydrangea, tree form
Sparkler Rose Cleome
Amazon Neon Purple Dianthus
Serena Blue Angelonia
Snow Crystals Alyssum

ZINNIA
EXPLOSION

The old-time Zinnia is enjoying a revival. Breeders are developing new colors in response to demand.

Zinnias are one of the few annuals which does best if seeded directly into the ground in mid-May.

If you purchase Zinnias in pacs, it is helpful to cut them back half-way at planting to allow the root to establish.

Zinnias often succumb to mold in mid-August. The problem can be minimized by watering them underneath, either by hand or with a soaker hose, rather than overhead with a sprinkler.

Zinnias come in a wild array of colors, and in shades from primary to pastel. The blooms can be double or single. The plants can be as short as six inches or as tall as four feet.

The zinnia fad is one that deserves to last for quite some time.

"Magellan Salmon™" zinnia

The new "Queeny Lime Orange" zinnia, an All-America selection here on trial at the University of Minnesota's West Central Research and Outreach Center in Morris, MN.

Several colors and styles of zinnia make a splash planted as a mass in Bergeson Gardens.

You can even plant zinnias that bloom green!

WHITE PAPER BIRCH

A native white birch in the Sand Hills near Fertile, M.N. Birch are often confused with aspen because both have white trunks. However, birch tend to grow in clumps, while aspen grow in parallel lines. And, as can be seen here, the outer branches of the white birch have a distinctive bronze tint, absent in aspen.

Just west of Enderlin, ND, is a grouping of Dakota Pinnacle® white birch, a popular NDSU introduction with a striking triangular shape.

After speaking at the Langdon, ND, city park, I headed across the prairie towards Grafton on North Dakota Highway 5.

A few miles east, the highway enters a short span of hills. One such hill sloped down to the highway from the south, and I did a double-take when I saw what was growing there.

Birch! Lots of them. Healthy, vigorous, and growing out in the middle of the open prairie where they usually don't volunteer to grow. But volunteer they did, because they found a north facing slope.

Birch in the woods in lake country in Minnesota appear in nature in the shade of north slopes, that much I knew. But I was surprised to find, out in the middle of North Dakota, some birch seed had somehow found a remote north slope, and there they took root.

We can learn a lesson from the birch east of Langdon.

White birch can be planted all across the northern prairie, but will succeed best where the soil is cool, such as the north side of buildings, or where larger trees shade the root. Unlike some trees, white birch benefit from automated sprinkler systems.

START SMALL

White birch are grown easily from seed and grow quickly from small seedlings into white-barked adolescence. Soil conservation services often carry small birch, either potted or bare root. The frailest looking string of a bare root birch will burst forth and multiply its size in the first season.

Larger birch—six feet or more—in pots are a poor investment as the root inevitably dries out, causing the entire tree to pout. Even when they live, they take several years to recover from the trauma to the root. Meanwhile, the stringy little seedling will pass the larger potted tree, both in height and general appearance.

In the wild, birch tend to grow in clumps, and many people prefer to plant 3-5 stems in a single hole to achieve the same effect in the yard.

If planted where the roots are kept cool, birch can live long lives in the northern prairie yard, contributing a touch of class with their chalky white trunks.

An innovative use of white birch on the north side of the Minneapolis Public Library. With their roots covered by slate and in the shade of a large building, these birch are set for a long life.

171

ARE WEEPING BIRCH HARDIER?

An odd discovery: Throughout the northern prairie, the weeping birch, which is a grafted cultivar of the white birch species, seems to be longer-lived and more adaptable to hostile soil conditions than the plain old white birch which grows in the wild in lake country to the east.

Further research reveals that the nursery trade at times bestows a Zone 2 hardiness rating on the weeping birch, while non-weeping white birch are are generally rated hardy for Zone 3.

The explanation may be very simple: the weeping birch's elegant curtain of branches, often left to trail to the ground, shades the root, keeping the soil beneath the tree cool. Hot, baking sun on the root is fatal to birch, and weeping birch may create enough shade to save themselves.

Because weeping birch are a *cultivar* that requires grafting and are likely to cost a minimum of $30 per stem, they are rarely clumped. That is not to say that one couldn't put three in the same hole.

Both trees feature the birch's chalky-white bark with black markings, as well as the bronze tinted outer branches, which give the birch winter interest.

This stately weeping birch just west of the tracks in Finley, ND, was planted 71 years ago, according to a woman who climbed its branches as a child.

ENGELMANN IVY
The Sturdiest Vine

An Engelmann Ivy climbs a trellis in Clark, SD.

For a perennial vine on the northern prairie, whether you want it to creep or climb, none is more hardy, attractive, or effective than the Engelmann Ivy, otherwise called woodbine.

It will grab a trellis, or perhaps just grab the cracks between the siding. It will climb a chimney or telephone pole. It will wander amongst big rocks, or hold a bank.

A native, Engelmann Ivy turn a bright red early in the fall, at which time they stand out in the woods amongst the still-green tree leaves.

Engelmann Ivy are vigorous, and can become a pest. They may be cut back nearly to ground level each year, an efficient way to keep them reasonably well-behaved.

An Engelmann Ivy shows its fall color in the wild near Fertile, MN.

This mix of heirloom variety tomatoes was raised by Sheila Capistran of Ada, MN.

TOMATOES
Our Summertime Favorite

Made especially tasty by our long hours of summer sunshine, tomatoes are probably our favorite northern prairie summertime treat.

To do their best, tomatoes need full sun—and air movement. To prevent disease, the plants can be staked, or raised above the ground with a cage. Grass clippings (as long as the lawn where they are obtained has not been sprayed) can be used as a mulch to prevent disease on the lower leaves.

Watering underneath, not overhead, also lessens blight. Prevention is more effective than fungicidal sprays.

The most common problem with tomatoes on the northern prairie is blossom end rot, which causes a big black circle at the bottom of the fruit.

Blossom end rot is entirely the product of inconsistent moisture. Once the plants get rolling in mid-June, tomatoes cannot be allowed to dry out even once or blossom end rot will manifest.

Tomatoes in pots are especially prone to drying out. Use large pots—the size of a whiskey barrel—to lessen the problem.

Although there are calcium sprays on the market which address blossom end rot, the calcium deficiency does not occur unless the tomato is allowed to dry out.

Just over 100 years ago, almost no deer were left on the northern prairie. The herd of white-tails in the entire state of Minnesota was estimated at fewer than one hundred. Over-hunting had nearly done them in.

"Unconfirmed sighting of deer reported," ran a front-page headline in a small-town paper in the Red River Valley in 1952, indicating that the population was still sparse mid-century.

Today, if you could prove that you have gone a week of normal living *without* seeing a deer, you might get in the local paper—if it hasn't gone extinct itself.

OH, DEER!
Facing the Menace

For those who plant trees, a high deer population means work. For every tree we plant, we must make provisions to protect it from the deer, or we're wasting time.

Yes, there are trees which the deer like *less*. Hackberry, buckeye, black walnut and maple come to mind. Cottonwood grow fast enough to eventually out-run the deer.

But *all* sapling trees are favorite places for the bucks to rub the velvet off their antlers in fall. Luckily, plastic tubing seems to deter them.

To establish two of our staple native trees, oak and basswood, or apples, another popular deer snack, we are going to have to protect against deer until the trees grow large enough for a majority of their leaves and limbs to be out of danger. A cage of wire or steel mesh is the only sure method.

It is now a fact of life: we prairie tree planters must be prepared to spend as much money on barriers to protect young trees from deer as we do on the trees themselves.

A doe peers into the author's living room.

DEER REPELLANT TIPS

Most all deer (and rabbit) repellants work well if applied properly. No matter the brand, they contain ammonia and animal fats and smell like a combination of rotten eggs and pig manure. The smell fades to the human nose within hours, but remains repulsive to the deer.

• Take care to apply the repellant to all of the foliage you do not want the deer to eat. Simply spraying the general area does not work as well.

• Spray about half-way to the point of dripping.

• Apply every ten days if there is no rain.

• Apply after a rain of more than ½ inch.

• Most spray nozzles will plug frequently with globules of fat and will need to be tapped clean. This is typical for deer repellant.

• Hosta, impatiens, apples and roses are the first things the deer eat. Start spraying the hosta as soon as they emerge from the ground, impatiens as soon as they are planted, and the apples and roses as they break bud.

• Fast-emerging new growth in June might require an additional round of spraying.

Hosta, such as this beautiful variety called "June," are particularly delicious to deer. If you have a deer problem, spraying the hosta foliage with deer repellant will keep the varmints from mowing them to the ground in one night.

AMMONIUM SULPHATE

How to apply ammonium sulphate on trees and shrubs...

Ammonium sulphate should be spread on the top of the soil. Never mix ammonium sulphate with soil at planting. Never pour ammonium sulphate in the bottom of the hole. Never use ammonium sulphate on potted plants.

Small bushes (2-4 feet): Use 1/4 cup, spread evenly in a two-foot wide area around the base of the shrub.

Large bushes (4-8 feet): Spread 1/2 cup in a four-foot wide circle.

Trees: Spread 1 cup per inch diameter of the tree's trunk beneath the canopy of the tree.

Ammonium sulphate may be applied any time, although if applied in the fall, spring moisture seems to bring the fertilizer to the roots in time for spring.

Apply once per year.

Application rate for flower and vegetable gardens:

1 lb. (two cups) per 50 square feet.

Ammonium sulphate loses very little potency if left on top of the ground for a while after application, but the sooner it is watered in, the better.

These chlorotic oak leaves in Vermillion, SD could be turned a dark green with an annual application of ammonium sulfate.

Why Ammonium Sulphate?

The ammonium part of ammonium sulphate provides nitrogen which all plants need for healthy, green growth.

The sulphate part of ammonium sulphate lowers the soil pH. Nearly all soils on the northern prairie have high pH, which ties up nutrients so the plants can't get them. Ammonium sulphate lowers pH and makes nutrients available.

Ammonium sulphate is particularly useful in soils low in humus.

Plants that are chlorotic (show yellowing of the foliage with darker green veins) can be greened up in a fairly short time with an application of ammonium sulphate.

PINE
A Nod to the Forests Flanking the Prairie

A row of windswept Scotch pine line the western edge of the cemetery of Faaberg Lutheran Church in tiny Rindal, MN.

Scotch Pine are
famous for their
orange bark.

The presence of native pine forests mark the east and west extents of the northern prairie.

One wishes more pine had been planted on the northern prairie itself over the past 100 years. Where they have been established, pine perform admirably, and should continue to do so with increased elegance and dignity for at least one hundred years more.

There are a few large groves of pine across the prairie planted in the 1940s and 1950s including an award-winning planting east of Mobridge, SD, which now qualifies as a small forest.

The Gary Pines, near Gary, MN, on the eastern fringe of the northern prairie, is now a rest stop where the prairie dweller can easily experience some of the defining pleasures of the mountain west: the low roar of wind through the needles, the rich forest scent, the dappled sunshine on the open forest floor. The trees were planted and maintained by a community-minded group of tree lovers in the 1940s, and their dream has been realized.

Several cities in the western half of the northern prairie, most notably Bismarck, have planted pine in their public spaces. May more cities follow suit.

A PINE PEST PREDICAMENT

"Pine wilt" disease is forcing us to re-think our pine tree planting ideas.

"Pine wilt" is a general term for an unholy alliance between a Sawyer beetle and a tiny worm known as a pinewood nematode. The beetle attacks the tree and introduces the worm. The microscopic worm quickly clogs up the pine's vascular system, killing the tree within months, or even weeks, leaving the dead needles to forlornly hang.

If you pass through Omaha on the interstate highway system, you will see that one out of about every dozen pine planted in the right-of-way are now dead.

The disease primarily attacks weak and stressed trees.

Good news: The Ponderosa pine, as well as a few lesser pine species native to the North American continent, are not susceptible to the worm.

Bad news: The Scotch pine, Austrian pine, and even the little Mugo pine, used in yard plantings, can get the worm.

Good news: The pine nematode worm requires a certain minimum summer temperature to live. The worm is prevalent in southern Minnesota and Wisconsin, and is established in southeast South Dakota, but has not made an appearance in North Dakota.

Bad news: The pine nematode is now in Watertown, SD, which is as far north as it has thus far been found on the northern prairie.

The obvious answer: plant only Ponderosa pine.

Prairie Pine Possibilities

So, what varieties should northern prairie pine proponents plant?

For large groupings, windbreaks, future forests, it is clear that Ponderosa pine are the way to go. In the higher elevations of western South Dakota, the lodgepole pine (Pinus contorta), also native to the continent and therefore immune to the nematode worm, is an alternative.

In the Zone 4 portions of the northern prairie, planting masses of Scotch pine is unwise due to the pine wilt disease. Yet, the tree is such a delight as a specimen, and has such unique attributes, that I hope we continue planting it in Zone 3, where the pinewood nematode has not yet arrived, and may never be a problem.

Planting Pine

Pine can be planted as small seedlings, or purchased in a pot. Larger potted pine (3-6 feet) have usually been trimmed into a tight, pleasing, Christmas-tree shape. That is fine, but such a formal shape simply cannot be maintained as the years progress.

Pine are best left to grow freely and develop their unique, often gnarled character. Plant them where they needn't be trimmed.

Bare root seedling pine should be planted deep enough so the soil brushes the lowest needles. Shallow planting can cause the exposed top of the young tree to dry out and die before the root has time to grab hold and supply moisture to the foliage.

NOSTALGIA FOR SCOTCH PINE

The loss of the Scotch (sometimes called "Scots") pine would hurt. I grew up with dozens of Scotch pine on our farm, trees Grandpa hoped to sell, but which kept growing to the point where they couldn't be moved.

Although nurserymen are trained to be heartless in grubbing unsold trees so they don't lose valuable land to excess inventory run amok, Grandpa couldn't bring himself to bulldoze the renegade rows of Scotch pine.

One Scotch had snapped off above ground level during a storm in the 1940s, only to regrow sideways for a few feet before heading skyward again. Grandpa made the tree the centerpiece of a hidden Zen garden which contained the gnarled pine and seven boulders evenly spread on pea rock.

I spent hours in that hidden space as a child, drawn by its tranquility without knowing why. The tree was taken down for a new building in the 1980s while I was away in college.

People love the orange bark of the Scotch pine. I loved climbing its open limbs as a kid. I enjoyed playing with the clear, sparkling drips of sap on the smooth trunk.

A single specimen still stands in our gardens, and it is a treasure. A few yards away are two pine which were part of a nursery row grown old. They are gnarled and elegant. I have mowed around them for 40 years!

I would hate to see the Scotch pine taken from us by fear of disease. Let us continue to plant the tree as a specimen in the northern half of the northern prairie.

These Scotch pine in Bergeson Gardens are what remains of a row originally intended for sale by the author's grandfather.

PINE VS. SPRUCE

Pine are distinguished from *spruce* by the length of their needle, which ranges from the 1-2 inch needles on the Scotch Pine (*Pinus sylvestris*), to the 3-5 inch needles of the Ponderosa (*Pinus ponderosa*), and even longer needles of the Austrian Pine (*Pinus nigra*).

As young trees, spruce are more prim in shape while pine are airy and open.

Unlike spruce, which become scruffy in their old age, pine simply become more elegant as the decades pass.

A Norway pine spotted in Harrisburg, SD. Minnesota's state tree is rarely seen west of the state's western border, and is not known to grow on the northern prairie. However, famed North Dakota horticulturist Neal Holland was fond of the tree and noted where specimens existed in his state. Neal taught the author how to instantly recognize a Norway pine: the boughs resemble human arms outstretched towards heaven, palms up. Neal Holland passed away in 2019. It would be appropriate to plant a few Norway pine in honor of his unquenchable optimism.

PONDERING
PONDEROSA
PINE

Ponderosa pine do not have the charm of the Scotch. They grow slender and straight, with lower limbs that aren't easy to climb. The young Ponderosa pine's bark is more black than orange, a trait I find drab.

But the more I travel the American west, the fonder I am of Ponderosa pine, the predominant pine in the mountains. They grow perfectly straight, eventually forming pillars of up to 100 feet or more.

As Ponderosa pine age, orange stripes appear on the deeply-grooved bark, in tandem with the deep black. If the Ponderosa is a bit plain in adolescence, it develops grandeur with age.

The slightest breeze through the Ponderosa needles raises a roar that can send shivers.

Due to its immunity to the pine wilt disease, Ponderosa are the prudent pine to plant.

A young Ponderosa pine planted on a golf course in Bismarck, ND

URBAN SPACES, URBAN GENES

It was June. The busy season had just ended, and it was time to order the geraniums for the next year to be certain we would get the varieties we wanted.

By the way, the sales person said, almost as an afterthought, the Sincerity geranium has been discontinued.

What? I was incredulous. Sincerity, with its bright orange-red blooms and vigorous growth, was our best selling geranium and had been for as long as I remembered.

"It just gets too big," said the company rep, with a shrug, not realizing how upsetting the news was to me.

It was my first lesson in how plant breeding and marketing works.

Yes, the Sincerity grew large and bloomed like crazy from top to bottom. That is what we want!

Turns, out that is just what most greenhouses did not want.

Sincerity grew so fast that the pots needed to be spread apart in April, or the plants would get leggy, weak, and perhaps diseased. With plenty of greenhouse space, that was no problem—for us.

But for urban greenhouses built on expensive real estate with limited space, the ideal geranium was one which stayed compact, and which put on a single big bloom by Mother's Day, when geraniums sell.

To replace the Sincerity, we were told we should move to the Tango, a prim little thing that stayed compact enough so no extra greenhouse space was needed.

But the Tango was not merely prim in the greenhouse. It stayed small throughout the growing season in the customer's pots. Customers used to the old-time vigorous geraniums were furious. My pots look empty! These things just don't grow!

Welcome to the world of ornamental plant genetics.

Breeding new plant varieties is big business—but it is a business, and breeders are primarily interested in creating new varieties which will sell in the big markets.

That would be the urban markets. And the urban market wants compact plants that bloom now.

Not only must a new plant fill the needs of urban customers, it must be attractive to the urban growers, who have limited greenhouse space on expensive land and need to turn a profit.

The same powerful market force also shapes the breeding of shrubs, trees and perennials. If you can attach the word "compact" to a new shrub or tree, you've got a winner. "Low-maintenance" is another popular buzzword for plants that never "get out of hand."

Indeed, the ideal urban tree or shrub seems to be one which grows in a strict geometric shape without trimming or pruning.

On the northern prairie, with our larger spaces and short growing season, we need some trees and plants which "get out of hand."

However, prairie planters are subjected to the urban media, and many of us adopt urban tastes and preferences without knowing why. In the process, we get snookered into buying plants we simply don't need, plants genetically stunted to suit urban spaces!

A rule of thumb for the prairie planter: When tempted by a highly-hyped, high-priced new plant that gets a lot of full-color free press thanks to a high-priced marketing firm, run the other way!

In the rare event that a highly-hyped new plant actually works, it will quickly become a staple. The price will come down. Buy it then.

Don't pay big money to be a guinea pig. And don't let urban aesthetics overwhelm your prairie sensibility.

AUTUMN BLAZE MAPLE

The Autumn Blaze maple blasted onto the prairie scene in the 1990s with great promise: It was fast-growing, shapely, and had a brilliant fall color. As a result, it was vigorously promoted and widely planted.

Too widely.

Today, the Autumn Blaze and its partner Freeman hybrids are struggling. At least half of them have died, or look sickly. Most prairie city forestry departments no longer recommend them for boulevards.

These two Autumn Blaze in Hillsboro, ND demonstrate the tree's problem in prairie soils: On one city block, the Autumn Blaze will do fine, on the next it will get sick and often die of iron chlorosis and winter bark damage.

The problem? Autumn Blaze balk at alkaline soils more than we thought. Many develop sickly yellow, even whitish leaves, a sign of iron chlorosis.

Furthermore, their trunks are subject to severe winter damage. Deep cold snaps the bark, and even can crack the trunk all the way through. Sunscald causes the bark on the south side of the trunk to die, creating an ugly and very damaging scar.

Yet, in every town there seems to be examples of the Autumn Blaze which are doing well, and experts aren't sure why.

What we do know is that fewer than half of the trees planted are healthy, and that the old-time sugar maple, although slower growing, is a better maple bet.

*An Autumn Blaze maple doing well on sandy soil in Fertile,
MN. Unfortunately, fewer than half of the Autumn Blaze planted
on the northern prairie succeed to this extent.*

SUGAR MAPLE

On sandier soils, the sugar maple turn deep orange-red in the fall, as it does here near Zion Lutheran church in Twin Valley, MN.

This sugar maple is doing well in Enderlin, ND, where it has the benefit of being on a slope. Any rise in ground level makes it easier to grow sugar maple on the northern prairie.

PYRAMIDAL ARBOR VITAE
A Prairie Sentinel

This row of pyramidal arbor vitae thrives in a yard in Miller, SD. Such rows do best in town, where arbor vitae seem less prone to winter burn.

This spectacular forest of pyramidal arbor vitae, most well over 80 years old, graces the cemetery in Ada, MN. Yes, the deer trimmed the bottom branches, but the trees still look grand.

The pyramidal arbor vitae is an immigrant to the prairie, a welcome source of winter green and a contributor of a column-like, biblical dignity to an otherwise horizontal landscape.

Once established, pyramidal arbor vitae have the ability to outlive us all. But for us to derive the maximum long-term effect from this useful tree, we should consider carefully where we plant it.

Given their neat upright appearance from an early age, many pyramidal arbor vitae are given the job of flanking the front steps of small homes, like a pair of soldiers standing at attention.

But the noble tree soldiers keep growing until their heads bang against the eves, a problem which is no fault of their own, but which has caused many homeowners to turn against the tree.

A better use of the pyramidal arbor vitae green soldiers is to post a pair flanking the family's grave stone, where, in theory at least, they can be allowed to grow as high as they wish.

For the yard, a grouping of pyramidal arbor vitae in a back corner left to grow to their heart's content is best.

Pyramidal arbor vitae do not thrive in all areas of the northern prairie, struggling where the winters are warmer and dryer. If you see a few old ones around town, plant one yourself.

BASSWOOD

No tree is as perfectly dependable for the boulevards and parks of northern prairie cities and towns than basswood, also known as linden.

The *species* American linden, (*Tilia americana)* is native to slopes near rivers on the eastern portion of the northern prairie. They can grow very large.

At our nursery, we once had a clumped basswood twice as wide in circumference at the base as the largest cottonwood!

Alas, the tree was killed by lightening. It took a D-9 Caterpillar to remove the stump.

*A more triangular variety of linden, possibly the
European, planted in Finley, ND*

COMPACT CULTIVARS

It is sometimes difficult to find plain old species American linden at nurseries, but cultivars of the American linden flood the market.

The justification for the existence of "improved" cultivars is always the shape of the crown. Trees of the species grow very large with a grand, wide-spreading crown, a characteristic which may be just what we need on the prairie, but which doesn't sit well with those planting in tight urban or suburban lots.

So, the market demands basswood which are more disciplined, whether they grow in a column, or an aggressive triangle shape, or in a tight oval.

In accord with market demands, the European Linden (*Tilia cordata*), sometimes referred to as "little-leaf" linden, have been introduced to the American market. A smaller tree, with a smaller leaf and a more aggressively geometric crown, the European linden, most notably the cultivar "Greenspire," contributes dignity to the urban landscape.
mower without the homeowner even having to bend over.

As soon as shoots appear at the base, rub them off with your hand rather than leaving them to grow until you need a clipper. The number of shoots will decline as the tree ages.

A Disease-Free Tree

Linden have no apparent disease problems. Once established, they are completely dependable.

Basswood are a favorite of bees, with their blooms producing the clearest honey available.

A stately row of linden on a berm in front of the Target in Watertown, SD.

So, what's there not to like? Well, American basswood leaves are large and leathery, which means they create a mess in the fall. The blooms drop during the summer, as do the seeds a while later. The branches are considered weak because the wood is so soft. Basswood also send up large numbers of suckers from the base.

So the old-time basswood has been tarred with the messy label.

Do not plant too deeply!

The only unhealthy linden out of the thousands I saw in cities across the northern prairie in the summer of 2019 was one planted too deeply, and with mulch piled against the trunk to a depth of five inches. Frequent watering had caused the mulch to rot the bark, and branches had begun to die.

Basswood, like maple, are extremely sensitive to being planted too deeply. The flare at the base of the tree's trunk which goes out to the root must be visible. Care must be taken at planting that the tree is not planted too deep. Improperly planted basswood don't limp along as some trees do—they get it over with and die right away.

Messy Schmessy

It is short-sighted to eliminate a tree from consideration because it drops a little more stuff than the next tree.

Whatever the basswood drops can be ground up with the average mower without the homeowner ever having to bend over.

As soon as shoots appear at the base, rub them off with your hand rather than leaving them to grow until you need a clipper. The number of shoots will decline as the tree ages.

How to Purchase Basswood

Basswood struggle to get started from seed, both in the wild, and in the nursery. First, basswood seed almost never germinate. Second, there are few trees whose branches and leaves are more delicious to deer. Third, as young trees, the species American linden refuse to grow straight, choosing instead to send their lead branch veering off to the side.

For that reason, only the most patient prairie tree planter should attempt to start basswood small. Instead, find trees in the seven foot range with a well-established leader. Protect the entire tree from the deer. Hang old CDs in the branches to ward off the woodpeckers, which love the basswood's sweet sap and will drill creepy-looking rows of holes to get at it.

A row of basswood along 8th Street in Moorhead, MN shows gold coloring on a somber fall day.

With a little work early on, one of the northern prairie's grandest native trees can be sent on its way to a self-sufficient adulthood of well over 100 years.

PROPER
TRUNK CARE
Preserve Your Young Trees
from Human Harm

Holding talks in over 100 city parks on the northern prairie enabled me to see up close the state of civic plantings. If I arrived early, I strolled around the park to see what trees, if any, were planted, and how they were doing.

Most parks were well-tended, and showed civic pride. Some parks were amply wooded already. Others were bare, with no sign that tree planting was on the agenda.

But a handful made me sad. I found several parks where an active tree-planting program was clearly in place, where a thoughtful variety of young trees had been planted, and were actively cared for—but where the young trees were being slowly but surely killed by improper care of the trunk.

Planting trees and then killing them is worse than planting nothing at all. A great amount of money and civic energy is expended, with no result. The risk is that the whole tree-planting endeavor will be discredited as a waste of time.

Fresh weed-trimmer damage to an Autumn Blaze maple, which is also suffering from cracked bark due to winter cold. The tree's prognosis is not good.

CARELESS CARE

The most damage humans do to young trees is with a weed trimmer.

I have wielded a weed trimmer, so I know how the mind of weed trimmer person works. You *must* get that last blade of grass growing near the trunk, so you nudge the whirring line as close as you can.

Oops! The weed trimmer nicked the bark. Oh well, so be it, trees can't be that tender!

They are. *Weed trimmers kill trees.*

That news has gotten out. The next move many have made is to protect the trunk from weed trimmers by putting tubes, screens, or wrapping around the base of the tree. Such protection serves the additional purpose of protecting young tree trunks from rodents and sun scald in the winter.

Here is the rub: trunk protection must be done before there is damage, or wrap and tubing do nothing but trap moisture against the bark and cause rot, compounding the original damage.

In one case, weed-trimmer damaged trees were wrapped tightly with a rubberized fabric. The fabric was wet. I folded the wrap back, and sure enough, the trunk was rotting at the point of injury. The outer branches of the tree were dying. The tree was doomed.

Trunk protectors *should not* be snug against the bark of the young tree. They should be rigid enough to allow air to reach the trunk. If the trunk protector presses against the bark in the least, it should be removed in summer.

Do all of that correctly, and what can happen? In one North Dakota city park that had properly protected trunks, the ants had filled up the space between the protector and the bark of the tree with soil up to one foot above ground level. Rain had turned the soil into mud, and sure enough, the bark was rotting. You can't win!

Yes, you can. But it takes thought, care and some time.

This tree is has been battling the weed trimmer for years, and is gallantly trying to recover. In the long term, it will probably die from structural weakness. Here is a case where a little herbicide goes a long way—killing the grass at the base of the tree will not harm the tree, and will keep the weed trimmer at a safe distance.

That brings us to yet another way humans kill trees while trying to help them: mulch.

Yes, mulch can keep the weeds down and prevent weed-trimmer damage. Yes, mulch can preserve moisture around young trees which do not receive regular water.

But mulch piled against the trunk is deadly. In one city park with about two dozen newly planted trees, nearly half of them had soaking wet mulch mounded against the trunk over six inches above the base of the tree. I pulled the mulch away, and the trunk was black, wet and rotting instead of gray and dry. Above, the tree was weak, with several dead branches.

To ensure that mulch doesn't do more harm than good, the mulch pile should look like a donut: mounded in a circle around the tree, but without any mulch piled against the trunk.

Just because in the Twins Cities they pile mulch against the trunk of nearly every young tree (they're killing them, but they refuse to change) doesn't mean we have to repeat the mistake!

Trunk care is essential for young trees, but it must be done right. Even the most well-intentioned attempt can go wrong if it isn't monitored.

Mulch around young trees should consist of organic matter that does not readily decompose. Shredded cedar bark is best. Mulching with fabric, plastic, rubber circles, as well as large rocks, does more harm than good. Several layers of newspaper provide a substitute for fabric that remains for about as long as it is needed.

TOO MUCH MULCH

Mulch piled deeply against the trunk of this basswood is causing rot, and the tree is showing dead branches above. The tree was planted too deeply as well. Recent research shows that trees planted too deeply suffer mightily in the long term.

New tree plantings need a caring human to continually evaluate what is working and what is not with trunk protection, and take action on the spot. There is no substitute, no gadget or method which does the job forever.

Trunk care is an ongoing battle.

But it is a battle that can be won. When the tree reaches late adolescence, and its bark turns corky, it should be on its own.

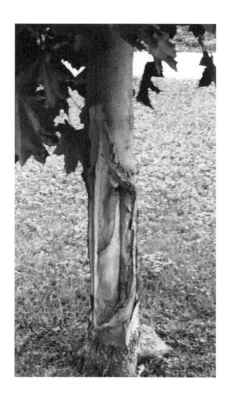

The trunk of this crimson-leafed Norway Maple has suffered years of winter sun scald damage, which could have been prevented with protective tubing or, as the trunk gets larger, a coating of white latex paint applied in fall. Norway maples and Japanese tree lilac keep smooth bark late into their life, and thus need protection from the sun even when their trunks get too large for the tubing.

This young Japanese Tree Lilac in Bismarck is getting an excess of care: The tubing is of the right kind, but would best be removed during summer. The mulch is keeping grass away, but is probably excessive. And, if freed from its shackles, the tree is not likely to escape. Staking is for trees with poor root systems that need help staying up while getting anchored. It need not be a routine practice.

A PLAN FOR TRUNK CARE

Trunks of young trees need protection up to the lowest branches for the first dozen or so years of their life.

The best protection is a screen, be it plastic or metal. Screen keeps away the rodents, foils the bucks, shades the trunk, and, if left on in summer, will discourage even the most determined weed trimmer.

Yet, screen lets the breeze flow through so the trunk is exposed to air, as it must be to be healthy.

The screen should be tied somewhat loosely to minimize contact with the trunk. When the tree matures enough to have rough, corky bark (the exact number of years varies between tree varieties), the protection should be removed.

The best way to prevent weed-trimmer damage is to keep the grass away from the trunk, either manually, or with herbicide (which will not hurt the tree as long as it is free of shoots growing from the base). With no grass near, the wielder of the weed-trimmer won't be tempted to toy with the tree's life in order to get that last blade of grass.

This protector is wrapped very tightly against the trunk. The trunk needs air, particularly in the summer. Tight wrapping does nothing to heal previous injuries.

THE VALUE OF
ARBORETUMS

One of my grandfather's unrealized dreams was to start a local arboretum. I never saw the practical value of such an undertaking, at least until I toured towns across the prairie.

An arboretum is simply a place where trees of all sorts are planted correctly, given the space to develop into specimens, cared for in their youth, and then observed for their fitness in the local climate.

Dr. Todd West, left, addresses part of the large crowd which attended the 2019 field day at NDSU's Horticultural Research Station near Absaraka, home of a large arboretum of experimental trees founded by Dr. Dale Herman.

An arboretum's failed attempts are as instructional as its successes.

Much to my surprise, many cities and towns across the northern prairie have long established arboretums, and many more cities are starting them.

Fast-growing Watford City, ND, has a nature park which is being lined with young trees, many of them introductions from North Dakota State University.

Yankton, SD, has placed an extensive arboretum along a well-used path. The city's Zone 5 climate allows for trees one would never see in parts north and west. The site is well worth a summer evening's stroll for visitors to the city.

The city park system in Sioux Falls is exemplary. At McKennan Park, there is the largest planted tamarack I have ever seen, as well as balsam fir, a true surprise.

We're supposed to regret importing the Siberian and Chinese elm, but look what this tree of that despised type developed into in a city park in Vermillion, SD.

223

ARBORETUMS BY OTHER NAMES

Not all arboretums need be designated as such. Dickinson's NDSU research experiment station, conveniently located within the southwest limits of the city, contains many acres of experimental trees, and is worth a lengthy visit. I drove through in a rainstorm and learned from their trial plots which of some less common trees do well in western North Dakota.

The NDSU horticultural experiment station near Absaraka, ND, is a tree-lover's paradise, and a tribute to its founder, Dr. Dale Herman.

This squirrel at SDSU's McCrory Gardens in Brookings, SD, had so many interesting trees to climb on it got tuckered out!

McCrory Gardens and the South Dakota State Arboretum are on the campus of SDSU in Brookings. Established tree plantings are combined with vast gardens of annuals and perennials in a pleasing and accessible layout.

The West Central Research and Outreach Center in Morris, MN not only features many experimental trees, but their staff plants and maintains a broad range of annual, perennial and vegetable gardens meant for the edification of the public. Their calendar is filled with public events, including a field day in late July which draws over 1,000 people annually.

I enjoyed walking the University of South Dakota campus in Vermillion, a treasure trove of uncommon shade trees such as the Kentucky Coffee Tree, a sycamore, even a few maturing American Chestnut.

The University of Minnesota-Crookston's campus has been thoughtfully beautified through tree planting for the past sixty years.

This Ohio Buckeye is one of many gracing the campus of the University of Minnesota-Crookston, worth a visit to see the tree plantings alone.

Two healthy baptisa (False indigo) at the NDSU Extension and Research station gardens in Dickinson.

225

A honeylocust shows its elegance at the cemetery north of Redfield, SD.

A FORWARD-LOOKING
PURPOSE FOR CEMETERIES

City cemeteries can double as an arboretum. Carrington, ND's stately cemetery is maintained with diligence, and contains several exemplary tree specimens. I spent a profitable half-hour in the cemetery in Redfield, SD. The cemetery in Ada, MN, contains stately examples of prairie trees.

Most old cemeteries are already arboretums, with specimens allowed to grow to maturity with a minimum of human interference—or, for that matter, help.

Perhaps at some point a town will consciously combine a cemetery with an arboretum, or a reclusive retired schoolteacher will leave a bunch of money designated for the purpose.

The work to create an arboretum is front-loaded: Unlike community flower beds, which must be maintained each year, an arboretum needs diligent care only in its early years. By the time the original committee dies off, as all committees do, the trees will be established.

To perform their role, trees in an arboretum must be labeled in a permanent fashion so passersby know exactly what they are looking at. Because labels tend to disappear, a detailed map, which includes the date of planting and the varieties should be kept at the library.

My trip to and through 100s of prairie towns showed me that each city grows a slightly different selection of trees. You simply can't predict which trees will work where. For that reason, each city, no matter how big or small, can profit by founding an arboretum where varieties new and old can be tried without risk of loss to any individual homeowner.

Grandpa was right. A small-town arboretum is a noble and useful project.

This fun-looking bush at the Ada Cemetery is simply a chokecherry, probably planted by birds, which, once it appeared, was merely trimmed up rather than being grubbed.

This disastrous planting somewhere in North Dakota has all the markings of a landscape contract that was adhered to literally ("trees will be staked with steel posts and wire of a gauge no less than…") but without the involvement of a human who actually cared. The dead juniper won't fall over, true, but that's small consolation.

STRIP MALLS AND PARKING LOTS
How Not to Landscape

Some of the least successful attempts at beautification through planting of trees and shrubs happen around the parking lots of businesses, institutions—and strip malls.

Recognizing the importance of softening up a bleak landscape, architects include nice blobs of green in their renderings of new buildings.

Those blobs rarely come to fruition.

Hoping to get it done right and for good, developers include a big, fat budget for trees and landscaping up front—with little thought for future maintenance. Their hope is that by spending up front they can lower costs later, as if they are putting in a top notch heating system.

Almost all of these attempts end in abject failure.

Working with living things requires gardening. That means perpetual care.

Rock looks good the day it is laid and goes downhill from there. It is a short-term solution and a long-term nightmare. Think how much better this area near a strip mall somewhere in North Dakota would look if it were just grass.

Here is a rare horticultural success in an institutional parking lot: Ivory Halo® dogwood left to grow without trimming at the Bismarck Municipal Ball Park. Ivory Halo is ideal for parking lot berms: It stays contained, but covers the ground well enough to suppress weeds.

S adly, the landscaping trade has succumbed to the allure of the first big dollars in the construction budget.

You can tell by the language the trade (I refuse to call it an "industry") has adopted: New landscapes are now "installed," and those installations include, almost as an afterthought, "plant materials."

Such obtuse language supports the notion that you plug plants in around a new building just as you would plug in a toaster.

Here are some ways the typical corporate mindset creates trouble:

For instant results, preferably before the grand opening, large trees are moved in with a spade. The trees are too large, but that is what big boss wanted, and here is a $50,000 budget to get it done.

Three-quarters of the tree's root is cut off by the spade, which means the tree will tip unless supported by a ugly scaffolding of stakes and wires.

Even if the tree somehow remains upright, it is stunted for the first several years by lack of root.

This planting of ornamental grasses at an institution somewhere in South Dakota was a good idea, but is being ruined by an automatic sprinkler system and excessive mulch. Ornamental grasses need neither.

Often the architect of a major building project, despite his lack of horticultural training, chooses the tree varieties to be planted. Of course, the architect is from a fancy firm at a big city in Zone 4 or 5.

I winced when I saw hundreds of non-hardy trees planted on the berms of an area convention center's parking lot. They are now all dead, the arena has no budget to replace them, and the parking lot looks bare.

Then there is the notion that using rock and and fabric around the plantings will prevent the need for future weeding or care. Rock may cover things up for a few years, but when the weeds bust through, and they will, you have a bigger problem than if you had done nothing.

Plus, scientific and anecdotal evidence is accumulating that rock and fabric kill shrubs and trees.

Finally, there is the notion that you can automate everything, including watering of the plants, and not have to worry about it.

Automatic watering systems kill trees. In recent years, automatic watering systems are also drowning the large plantings of ornamental grasses that have become popular in corporate plantings.

Wanting instant trees, the developer of this property somewhere in North Dakota purchased trees with lots of top and little root. Not even the stakes can keep it straight! Very few trees recover from such an awful start.

You need a *human* to decide when to water!

I am sorry, corporate barons, you can't get rid of the human element, the need for a nurturing gardener *somewhere* on your payroll.

Such humans are difficult to find, and they usually aren't motivated by money.

So, what is the corporate office to do?

If no candidates step forward, *plant grass*.

Lawn is a perfect fit for the corporate mind. You can water lawns automatically. You can hire a lawn service to do the mowing and upkeep.

Organizations which demand a low cost and low maintenance landscape had best plant grass and leave it at that.

This barberry in a new corporate planting on a parking lot berm somewhere in North Dakota was doomed from the beginning. First, most shrubs don't like to grow in rock. Second, barberry require the snow cover which comes from being right next to a house. Even if it had lived, this dwarf red barberry would have been too small to make an impact on this large-scale landscape.

GOLDSTURM
RUBDECKIA

Often referred to as "black-eyed Susan," the rudbeckia is best planted in a naturalized mass which echoes how it might occur in nature. The "Goldsturm" grows to three feet, and blooms enthusiastically for most of the summer, even if shaded for up to one-third of the day. According to Neal Holland, it survives eight out of ten prairie winters, so should be considered a short-lived perennial. It makes up for that deficiency by blooming like crazy for a longer portion of summer than most perennials.

COLEUS

A single plant of the new sun-tolerant coleus dominates
this bed of large annuals. The coleus is thriving in peat,
but has the benefit of some spectacular genetic
advances that have moved coleus from a novelty plant
for indoors or outdoor shade into a strong structural
addition to large flower beds in full sun.

HONEYBERRY

Dubbed the "blueberry of the prairie," the honeyberry works well in the northern prairie soils and climate where the blueberry itself simply does not. Comparisons with blueberry end with the coloration of the fruit, for the honeyberry has a flavor and texture uniquely its own.

Honeyberries ripen in early June, which makes them a favorite of birds. To avoid losing your crop to avian raiders, cover the bushes with a net.

Honeyberries must be pollinated by a different variety of honeyberry. Nurseries which sell the plants are generally expert on the matter. New varieties are being introduced annually as enthusiasm for this tasty fruit quickly grows.

It is difficult to tell when the honeyberries are ripe, as they turn dark blue long before they are ready for picking. To sort out the ripe from the unripe, harvest the fruit by shaking the bush gently over a cardboard tray.

The fruits are good for syrup and jams at any stage of ripeness.

ELDERBERRY

A rarity: a fruit that thrives in low, soggy ground. The native elderberry forms clusters of purplish-blue berries on a six-to-eight foot, rank-growing shrub which can double as an ornamental screen.

The shrub will die back some winters, but will recover with new growth almost immediately the next summer.

Lack of familiarity with the fruit leads many to believe it isn't edible. In fact, elderberry are very good, both for eating off the bush and for syrups, jellies and wine.

"TOBA" HAWTHORNE

Developed in Manitoba, the "Toba" is the hardiest hawthorne, and has grown well across the northern prairie. Its white blooms turn pink before dropping, and the red fruit, edible by birds, provides fall interest. The twisted trunk, shown here on a tree spotted in Bismarck, is characteristic of the mature tree. The above speciman in Hillsboro, ND, is thriving in Zone 3 on the heaviest of soils.

THE BEST DWARF SPIREA

Dwarf spirea are used so frequently in professionally designed corporate and home plantings that one might be forgiven for getting tired of them.

The "Tor" spirea, however, is increasing in popularity for its hardiness, prim shape, and spectacular fall color. During the winter of 2018-2019, many spirea suffered winter damage which required harsh spring pruning. Not so the Tor, which came through virtually unscathed.

247

CHERRIES FOR THE PRAIRIE

Thanks to our Canadian neighbors on the Alberta prairie, we have more hardy cherries to choose from all of the time.

If you prefer a small tree, the Bali (known as "Evans" in Canada) produces bright red berries which are set off by glossy, dark green foliage, giving the tree ornamental value in addition to its role in making top-notch cherry pie.

Cherries grown as a bush seem to last longer. The Carmine Jewel™, (pictured right), a variety only recently introduced south of the border, features darker fruit on a shrub which grows to six feet tall.

Bali Cherry

All prairie cherries, whether in tree or shrub form, should be netted well before the fruit begins to ripen or the birds will take the fruit green.

Cherries for the prairie seem to pollinate themselves just fine without the need for an additional bush.

The Carmine Jewel™

PEONIES

Peonies are a traditional and extremely sturdy perennial for the northern prairie. Their mid-June bloom brightens summer before annual flowers reach peak bloom.

Although the roots can be expensive, the plant lasts forever once established. Take care not to plant too deeply, or they will not bloom. Adding bone meal to the soil before planting provides needed phosphate for the life of the plant.

The stunning and sturdy Bartzella Peony
justifies its high price with a week-long June
bloom at a time when we could use some color.

251

WILL THE SUCCULENT FAD LAST?

Succulents are all the rage, and the fashion has spread from more populated regions of the country to the northern prairie.

Unfortunately, the clever and beguiling succulent arrangements aren't going to last on the northern prairie, as we lack the intense heat and year-around sunshine for them to thrive long-term.

A succulent arrangement in the house is probably the best. Succulents are slow to decline, but decline they will, so it is best to regard the arrangement as temporary.

For those who wish for succulents outdoors, stick to sedum and the hardier varieties of Hen and Chicks (Sempervivum) and you will have years of fun. Plant them in the hottest, driest spot you can find.

A nod to the current succulent craze in a stately planter at Munsinger Clemens Gardens in St. Cloud, MN.

PRINCESS KAY
FLOWERING
PLUM

The first tree to bloom in spring, with blossoms that start white and turn light pink, the Princess Kay, discovered in the wild in Itasca County, Minnesota, bears no fruit and will never exceed twelve feet in height. The leaves can turn reddish in the fall. The tree does best where it never sits wet, as the root will rot and the tree will simply fall over.

BLACK WALNUT

There is archaeological evidence that Black Walnut were once the predominant tree along the Red River of the North. Today, there are some large specimens as far north as Grand Forks.

Black walnut are lightly sprinkled through towns across the northern prairie, and where I saw them, they were healthy, showing no signs of struggle against the elements.

One argument against planting black walnut is their slow rate of growth. But remember, slow growing trees are long-lived, high quality trees, and the black walnut is both.

Black walnut develop an upright crown but are airy enough to be more elegant than formal.

A Poison Problem?

In addition, there is the matter of *juglone,* a poison produced by the black walnut, which renders the soil around the tree toxic to certain shrubs and flowers. The effect of the poison lasts for years after the tree is removed.

The poisonous effects of black walnut trees are far worse in areas where the tree grows huge. Sioux Falls, Vermillion and Yankton, SD, are the only likely places on the northern prairie where the black walnut will grow to a size that will poison large areas of a yard. To the west and the north, I did not see or hear of a problem.

Indeed, you can find online lists of shrubs and plants which are not hindered by the poison. Prominently included on the list are hydrangea.

A Quality Tree With Benefits

For those of us on the northern prairie who have wide open expanses and relatively large yards, it is likely that we can find a place for this elegant, storied tree.

Oh, and black walnut trees produce walnuts. Sometimes by the bushel, to the point where a few people consider them a nuisance. Yes, you can eat them—if you can crack them! (A bench vise works best.)

A Long-Term Treasure

A few years ago, long-time nursery customer Jim Benoit of Red Lake Falls, MN, presented our family with a plaque carved with a tribute to my grandparents, parents, and my brother and I. The plaque consisted of a slab of black walnut taken from a tree he had purchased from Grandpa, which had to be sawn down.

The wood was beautiful, and the plaque a keepsake.

Yes, we can grow black walnut, and yes, if they are so inclined, our descendants can use it to make beautiful locally-grown furniture.

Yes, the black walnut produce nuts, and yes, they are edible!

Black walnut's large leaf fronds turn a striking golden yellow on the northern prairie.

257

COTTONWOOD

What would the northern prairie be without the big old cottonwood, the wooly mammoth of trees?

A lot less poetic, that's for sure. As much mess as a cottonwood tree creates when growing in a yard, no tree is more loved by prairie dwellers, for no prairie tree sticks in the memory like the cottonwood.

My great-grandmother, Emma Johnson, planted about twenty cottonwood on our farm circa 1905. Old photos reveal their progress from slender, fast-growing saplings to sturdy pillars.

When our young family moved from suburbia back to the small town in 1969, the neighbor men gathered to wave their arms and offer advice as Dad wormed our 70-foot trailer into a spot between three of the massive cottonwood trunks.

Unsafe, yes, but we did a lot of unwise things back then and survived them all.

A lone old cottonwood in the Sandhills near Fertile, MN.

CHILDHOOD
MEMORIES

The trailer had no air conditioning, so I laid
in bed under an open window on stagnant
summer nights and waited for the
cottonwood leaves to announce the arrival
of the slightest breeze with a crisp racket.
Even a few drops of rain on the rubbery
cottonwood leaves made a crackling, rat-a-
tat sound.

I mowed around the cottonwood, made a
tree house in one, hung a swing from
another. And it was my job to pick up all the
branches which fell during windstorms. I
can still smell the sticky sap on my hands.

October! The cottonwood leaves turned
butter yellow. On a sunny Sunday, the
reflected light filled the trailer, filled the
yard, warmed the soul enough to make up
for another heartbreaking Vikings' loss.

All good things must end...

A storm flattened all but one of great-
grandma's cottonwoods in August of 1987.
Although Grandma and Grandpa's house
was only slightly damaged by the falling
trees, Grandpa announced "This isn't home
any more," and joined Grandma in the
nursing home.

*This lone cottonwood northeast of Rothsay, MN, is
a favorite of many northwest Minnesotans who pass
by it on the way to Minneapolis. Photo by Adele
Spidal, a fan of the tree.*

It took us years to get around to cleaning up the mess. We finished the job in 1993, and after spending one season just looking at the open space, decided to turn it into a garden, which it is today.

As popular as the gardens have become, I'd rather have the cottonwoods back.

By modern safety standards, an old cottonwood is a hazard. A dead ten-foot leg-sized limb from on high once stabbed itself deep into our lawn, and Dad let it stand for a few weeks as a lesson to all.

Cottonwood are a country tree, not a town tree. Their roots plug sewer lines, lift sidewalks, and bust up foundations of homes. So, the cottonwood doesn't make the city forestry department's list of suggested trees.

This home midway between Mankato and Worthington, MN is graced with stately trunks of old cottonwood, which soar above the yard like the pillars of a cathedral.

But when the town square is graced by a big old cottonwood, pity the city official who proposes cutting the mammoth down! That's one council meeting the mayor will find a reason to skip.

They're not a town tree, but nothing is so grand as the cottonwood pillars which soar like cathedral arches above so many prairie town parks.

So, against all usual common sense, I say let them stand! And, as a pro-cottonwood radical, I say: Let's plant more!

Cottonwood will always occur naturally in the country, whether as grand solo specimens in a field, massive forests in the river bottoms, or volunteers which line an old twin-rut drive.

But some rebels actually plant cottonwood on their lot in town. As long as they plant them far from sewer lines and the house, why not?

Indeed, because cottonwood are able to survive drought better than other trees, even better than the seedless faster-growing cottonwood hybrids, the old-time species cottonwood are often the best option for towns on the arid western reaches of the northern prairie.

GROW YOUR OWN WILLOW AND COTTONWOOD

Two old-time prairie stalwarts, willow and cottonwood (and hybrid variants), can be started easily by cuttings by the homeowner.

Cuttings must be taken from last year's growth. Ideally, the shoot grew vigorously, adding at least four feet of growth.

To prepare for taking cuttings, one might cut back a sapling in the wild so it produces a bunch of fresh shoots, which can easily be turned into dozens of cuttings early the next winter.

Harvest the slender, whip-like branches before the snow melts. Cut them into foot-long lengths. Discard cuttings thicker than one's thumb or thinner than a pencil. Store the cuttings in a plastic bag in the fridge until planting time.

264

The cuttings can be planted in May in ground that has been deeply tilled. The addition of sedge peat tilled to the depth of one foot really gives cuttings a boost.

Cuttings can be planted as close as two inches apart. Press the cutting *all the way in the ground*. Only the very tip of the cutting need be visible, and if that is covered with a light film of soil, no harm is done. Plant in a row, or in a grid. Water as you would anything else throughout the summer.

Cottonwood cuttings usually grow from ground level to 5-7 feet in the first season. Willow can grow to 2-3 feet. The trees can easily be dug up and moved to their home location early the next spring.

TURF BATTLES

"How do I get rid of white clover in my lawn?" asked a lady in Watertown, SD. "My neighbor says I need to get rid of it before it spreads into his lawn."

Oh, boy.

First, white clover is about as good a lawn plant as grass itself. It is a delight to mow, and its little white flowers are fragrant and good for the bees.

Second, the notion that a neighbor with non-grass plants in their lawn, or even bad weeds, is going to make *your* lawn weedy, is nuts. Every lawn contains weed seeds by the thousand. They remain viable for years.

It is the *conditions you create*—lack of water or fertilizer, unwise mowing practices— which allow the weed seeds to germinate and thrive, not the mere presence of the seeds.

The bottom line: one weedy lawn in the neighborhood *does next to nothing* to increase the possibility of weeds in neighboring lawns.

"But, I just hate those little white flowers!" said another lady in a different part of South Dakota.

What has darkened your heart to the point where you hate little white flowers?

This lawn at Bergeson Gardens is full of non-grass plants such as clover. It is never sprayed for weeds, but is watered regularly and occasionally fertilized.

The chemicals used to eradicate those last non-grass plants are some of the worst we have. Their fumes get up and move after they are sprayed and damage—or even kill—shrubs, trees, flowers and vegetables. When used on home lawns, those chemicals simply are going to come in contact with children, pets—and you.

But the prevailing dogma, particularly in suburban areas, is that decent citizens must, to quote a box store advertisement for lawn chemicals, "show your yard who's boss."

"May the best lawn win," says a determined man in another advertisement, in which career-aged males glower at each other from their suburban turfs, pondering how best to win the perfect lawn competition.

In a bizarre twist in yet another ad, a man plays catch with his teenage daughter, but is distracted by daydreams of pouring more chemical on his lawn.

A close examination of this lawn would reveal ample clover, many dandelions—as well as some Creeping Charlie.

The teenage daughter, who through some miracle has no phone and is willing to be seen with her father in public, rolls her eyes at her Dad's obsession.

So should we all.

Mow, water, fertilize, and grass will prevail in your lawn, even when it wasn't seeded in the first place.

The perfect all-grass lawn does not happen in nature. The quest for it arises from a destructive and ever-worsening fad fueled by shame-based advertising that equates a dandelion in the lawn with bad breath.

To quote the writer Michael Pollan, "a lawn is nature under totalitarian rule."

Get a tattoo. Pierce your belly button. Grow a shaggy beard that draws fleas. But when it comes to your lawn, avoid the prevailing fads and let nothing govern your actions but good sense.

TOWARDS A NORTHERN PRAIRIE AESTHETIC

I arrived at the Split Rock Park in Garretson, SD over an hour early. After a brief tour of Garretson's beautiful park on the banks of the Split Rock river, I decided to sneak away for a bit.

Garretson resident Lisa Halverson had invited me to visit her yard a few miles west of town. I usually turn down such invitations due to time constraints, but Lisa had some plants to show me that were purchased at Bergeson Nursery, so vanity got the best of me.

I had all of twenty-five minutes. Riding on the back of Lisa's ATV, I got a quick tour of her scenic acreage, situated on the banks of the Split Rock River, which has carved stunning, mostly hidden, gorges in the quartzite bedrock prevalent in far eastern South Dakota.

Lisa has spent 30 years developing the acres on her side of the river into what I quickly realized was a classic example of tasteful northern prairie landscaping.

The trees on this beautiful hillside near Fertile, MN, were planted by the late Chuck Erickson, and show what beauty can result from the seemingly random placement of a variety of trees. Imagine if Chuck had used rows!

Although her vegetable gardens are neat and formal, the outlying areas along the river displayed a philosophy I would describe as "the embellished natural landscape." Lisa took what was there and added trees, shrubs and flowers in a manner which might fool you into thinking it just happened that way.

The twenty-five minutes spent in Lisa's domain spurred hours of thought: Just what is our goal in northern prairie yard design? What works? What fails? Do we have a coherent philosophy, or are we just winging it?

How much do we need to borrow from other areas of the country and world? What do we have that others might borrow?

A little philosophy...

The ancient Greeks considered the question "What is beautiful?" to be of profound philosophical importance. They labeled the study of beauty "aesthetics," and debated the matter endlessly.

Later, in Europe, gardening became a passion—as did philosophizing in journals, magazines and newspapers about what constitutes a beautiful garden.

Many prairie gardeners might be taken aback at the notion that their yard constitutes a philosophical statement. Yet, it does.

Matters of taste...

Formal or informal? Shaped or sprawling? Wild or tame? Native or exotic?

These issues are worth discussing, if we can do so with civility and a sense of humor.

Doing so would help us realize that beauty in a yard, garden or park is not a fixed concept. Everybody has their own opinions, and while I don't concede that all opinions are of equal merit, it is worthwhile to hear other views and dig into why we value what we do.

Thirty years ago, Lisa Halverson planted this Prairie Cascade weeping willow on the bank of the Split Rock River. Today, it looks as if it happened naturally. On the left is an Adam's Flowering Crab, planted in honor of Lisa's son of the same name.

Motives...

The first question to ask before launching into a yard project is, "Why am I doing this?" If the answer is, "I just want my yard to look nice," the next question is: "What do you mean by *nice?*"

"What are most people doing these days?" asked a customer who had come to me for landscape design help in preparation for an upcoming graduation. "I want to know what people are doing."

Her main motive in dolling up her yard: to be fashionable. She had no interest in gardening until it became necessary to put on an acceptable graduation party. Her utmost desire for her yard was that it conform to what "people are doing," and that it do so by next week.

Well, I had little sympathy. My "the customer is always right" philosophy fell apart.

"You can do what most people are doing, but what most people are doing is simply nuts!" I said, thinking of the rock, fabric, edging, and little round bowling ball shrubs that typically make up instant landscapes.

"What you want is a landscape that will make you happy for decades, not just for graduation!"

No, she did not want that. She went elsewhere. And I started to wonder if I was suited for the nursery business.

Where do we get our ideas?

Many of our aspirations for our yards and gardens come from elsewhere. We see a beautiful yard filled with rhododendrons and blue hydrangea in Seattle, and we want one here. We see a magnificent spread in a magazine of a Georgia spring bloom, and we want it here. We see a formal garden at a castle in Europe, and we want one here.

But what is beautiful *on the northern prairie?*

Rather than bemoaning what they have and we can't, perhaps we can look at what we have that they don't.

Northern prairie assets...

What do we have? Plenty.

Open spaces. Huge vistas. Windswept grasslands. Prairie plants. Large yards. Intense and lengthy summer sunshine, followed by grand sunsets. Often glorious autumns. A sense of solitude.

How can we enhance our advantages through our planting practices rather than trying to be something we are not?

For instance, gazebos...

A classic example of an imported idea of dubious merit: the gazebo. Obviously of southern origin, the romantic doll-house ideal is that you amble out in your petticoats with your beau and sit in the gazebo's shade and sip a mint julep on a hot afternoon.

Such a movie scene seldom develops amongst prairie folk, and it feels forced when it does. The northern prairie work ethic soon kicks in, the petticoats get tossed aside, and we start weeding, watering, trimming or mowing.

Now *that* feels good!

A PRAIRIE ALTERNATIVE TO GAZEBOS

Red monarda, a variant of a native prairie plant, have naturalized into a mass which makes this old building on Lisa Halverson's property look more nostalgic than shabby.

Northern prairie towns and farmyards are filled with old buildings which nobody tears down because nobody needs the land that badly. Can we make them beautifully nostalgic rather than junky and dowdy?

I once snuck onto an abandoned farmstead to explore a striking old tin granary that will never be used again. Inside, the sun came through a small four-pane window in the peak and bounced around the wood trusses. On the bare wood pillars were written in big fat pencil the bushels of oats and wheat harvested in 1947, 1948, 1949. In the bin, traces of decades-old grain.

The south side of the tin building was hot, ideal for a planting of hardy grapes, which could climb the high wall to their hearts content, or some old-fashioned roses. Against the north wall, a mass of bridal wreath spirea. On the east, a bleeding heart, perhaps a clematis.

With a little care, the old tin granary could have been the perfect northern prairie yard feature: historic, nostalgic, industrious, an ideal place to sneak away from the hubbub in the house for a smoke and a nip of brandy.

I guess we don't do that anymore. But you can bet our forefathers and mothers did!

And you can bet that none of them had a gazebo.

277

BEGINNINGS OF A PRAIRIE AESTHETIC

Our prairie climate and heritage points us in certain design directions, a few of which I will list. These points should be considered a starting point for thought and discussion, not dogmas. Some are in response to what I saw traveling the prairie in the summer of 2019.

• Emphasize native trees. Bur oak, cottonwood, basswood, black walnut and willow have been a part of the prairie for millennia. They are our palette. They look natural. They are part of our history. And they work. The oak savannah prairie landscape is ours alone. Let's rebuild it in ways big and small.

• Emphasize hardy fruits. We can get everything we need at the store, I know. But there is a purpose and a beauty to raising plants which were once meant for mere survival. It warms the soul to create beautiful plantings with a serious purpose, and it is deeply satisfying to see them succeed.

• The most useful purpose of decorative yard plantings on the prairie is to soften, to calm, to protect, to give the scene the feeling of falling asleep under a heavy old quilt. Tuck things in corners. Screen the cold, bare grain bin. Create little refuges and nooks. Make visitors who drive up feel they are coming in from the cold even before they step out of the car.

• Plan decorative plantings to provide memorable moments throughout the four seasons, remembering that each plant has its season, and on the prairie that season is short, but intense. Flowering crab bloom in mid-May, lilacs later in the month. Peony and iris do their thing in June. Most perennials bloom in July. Apples show up in August. Make sure your yard has something fun to visit each month.

• Don't forget to plant to improve winter. A cluster of pine on the edge of the yard earns its worth if you simply stand under it and listen to the wind through the needles once per winter. The branches of Flame Willow visible across the yard from the kitchen sink glow in the late winter sunshine, brightening dull March. A fresh snowfall on the boughs of a spruce makes Christmas cozy. Berries on the flowering crab draw birds.

• The most pleasing prairie landscapings are those which betray only a moderate level of human involvement after planting. Tightly trimmed hedges, shrubs and trees can be overbearing rather than calming, creating an off-putting sense that the priority of the gardener is control.

• On the opposite end of the spectrum, untended plantings are worse than no plantings at all. If you aren't going to weed it, don't plant it. A tidy lawn with no plantings is better than plantings gone to heck.

• It is not prudent to break up every wide-open prairie yard with island flower beds, or trees placed with no other purpose than to fill space. Although we needn't require each tree to write up a mission statement, it is good for a tree to serve a discernible purpose. Shading the deck. Blocking a view. Drawing birds. Screening a mess. It seems that adding trees one-by-one, each intended to serve a specific purpose no matter what it might be, creates a handsome landscape over the years more effectively than a massive plan laid out the first year.

Those who have planned a new house know it's guaranteed that in two years you will have no idea why you put the light switches where you did. The same holds true for trees and shrubs. Add them over time as you feel inspired for more satisfying long-term results.

A dwarf blue spruce combines with some naturalized rudbeckia and echinacea to embellish the natural landscape along the Split Rock River on Lisa Halverson's property.

NATURALIZING

Many prairie perennials, especially ones of native origin, will *naturalize*, that is, they will overtake small areas. Monarda spread, and that is natural. Some ornamental grasses widen their territory. So do rudbeckia, and certain coneflowers. *Let them.* Nothing is quite so pleasing as a mass of attractive plants that looks like it just showed up!

THE MATTER OF ROWS

• Rows of shrubs or trees should be avoided unless there is an obvious purpose for having them in a row, such as delineating a property line, blocking off the neighbor's collection of rusting cars, stopping the wind, protecting from dust, or creating a grand green wall at the rear of the lot.

• *Shrubs* planted in rows as a hedge should always be close enough to appear as one continuous blob of green, whereas *trees* in rows should be far enough apart (thirty feet) to maintain their individual dignity. The exception is shelterbelts, where trees can be placed as close together as ten feet in order to create an effective wall.

• Shrubs should not be spread singly around the lawn, or in a widely spaced row with grass in between. I have yet to see this practice work. It looks like the kids left the toys out.

This row of Norway Poplar planted along the author's driveway suffered one casualty. Now there's a gap. Does it matter? Not really.

• Rows should never alternate varieties of trees or shrubs. Start a different row for each variety, or simply place the additional varieties in groupings if you lack the room for a complete additional row.

• Not all trees work in rows. Ohio Buckeye, stubbornly individualistic trees, look crimped and miserable in a row, mad that they have to stand in line to get lunch. Hybrid poplar in rows, meanwhile, stand proud like soldiers in review. Birch look better in clumps than rows.

• If a long row of trees or shrubs runs through a low spot which causes a stretch of the plants to be stunted, grub out the weak ones and leave a gap rather than hope they'll catch up. They won't. And a gap in a row isn't the disaster it might seem. Trees aren't teeth. shrubs, cut back the old deciduous shrubs, clean up the trunks of the old trees, then back away for a couple of months to see which you like and which needs to go.

The critical ingredient...

The quality which most describes a successful northern prairie landscape is *thoughtfulness.* Unfortunately, I don't think it works to hire somebody to do that thinking for you. It has to spring from within, and it takes time to develop one's thoughts.

So too, it takes time for a beautiful landscape to unfold. The most beautiful yards happen when the person and the landscape grow up together. These yards, like life itself, reach peak richness in their 50s and 60s.

284

USE WHAT IS GIVEN YOU

Renovating an old, over-grown yard? Prune up the old evergreen shrubs, cut back the old deciduous shrubs, clean up the trunks of the old trees, then back away for a couple of months to see which you like and which needs to go.

Seldom is it necessary to start completely over, and often the old plants can stick around for a few years to give the new plants a start.

A large scale bed with a castor bean, a Sutherland Gold elderberry, impatiens and Baby Tut® ornamental grass.

It is very unusual to see a completely healthy Norway Maple as far north as this one grows in Garrison, ND. But it can happen! The homeowner protected the trunk in winter and removed the tubing for summer, which is crucial.

MICROCLIMATES

Although the soils and climate of the northern prairie are (at least for horticultural purposes) roughly uniform across a massive swath of this country's interior, geographic features sometimes create a microclimate where odd things happen.

Bismarck, North Dakota can be considered a northern prairie tree paradise. All trees rated hardy to Zone 3 and 4 do well there, probably due to the river-bottom soils and surrounding bluffs.

Just east of the Missouri River in South Dakota, meanwhile, moisture seems unusually scarce and the soils are mercilessly alkaline. Even the toughest trees show signs of long-term stress.

Meanwhile, the strip of prairie between I-29 and the South Dakota-Minnesota border gets more rain than any other region of the northern prairie, which means bigger trees and a lush landscape, but more fungal diseases on spruce, flowering crab, roses and apples.

Garrison, North Dakota, is highly alkaline, but supports some Zone 4 trees, such as honeylocust, which usually thrive further south but appear healthy in Garrison.

In Hazen, a few miles south of Garrison as the crow flies across Lake Sakakawea, honeylocust showed signs of severe winter damage. Go figure.

These seemingly slight differences mean that the savvy tree planter will, before selecting varieties of trees to plant, drive around and take a look at what is already growing well in the immediate area.

FROM ABERDEEN
TO ZAP

From the meeting room at the Aberdeen, SD public library you can see one of the many Victorian homes in the city, many of them with round corner turrets.

I scheduled Zap last on the tour of fifty North Dakota cities for reasons more alphabetic than logical. Despite having to rush from Bowman, ND due to time zone confusion, it worked out well.

A lively crowd of over twenty met me at the Zap city park picnic shelter. The group included several who had attended earlier talks, as well as one couple who drove four hours from Park Rapids, MN just for the heck of it!

It was a satisfying end to the North Dakota part of the tour.

After the talk ended, there was still plenty of summer sunlight to light my drive across some of the grandest prairie vistas you'll ever see.

In keeping with the alphabetic theme, one of the first stops last spring was the Aberdeen, SD public library. It was my first trip to the busy prairie city with a great collection of Victorian homes.

Signing a Successful Gardening book in Zap, ND

It is one thing to drive across the prairie on the freeway. It is another get a little insight into more than 100 prairie towns by visiting the library, or speaking at the park picnic shelter, and visiting with the locals.

Even planning the tour and finding locations to speak was a learning experience, and helped me meet so many kind, helpful and interesting people.

Memories of the *Successful Gardening* summer tour will enrich me for a long time.

Thank you all!

Successful Gardening on the Northern Prairie is the first complete yard and garden guide specifically for the cold climate and alkaline soils of the northern prairies of western Minnesota, North and South Dakota, as well as eastern Montana. Presenting the basics of prairie planting of trees, shrubs, fruits, annuals, perennials and vegetables, Successful Gardening is sure to make a difference for gardeners of every level of experience. Published in 2017, Successful Gardening has sold more than 15,000 copies and will soon enter its fourth printing.

Purchase at www.ericbergeson.com.

A Treasury of Old Souls is a collection of engaging stories about Eric Bergeson's lifetime spent amongst a small town's aging population. Even as a young child, Eric found himself in friendships with people in their golden years. In mid-life, he realized that his own perspective on life, death and relationships had been powerfully shaped by these unique friendships. Poignant, funny, yet gently instructional, Treasury is masterfully told in Eric's signature entertaining style as he traces the growth of his love and understanding of the elderly from his first day of kindergarten to recent adventures with his centenarian great aunt Olive. Treasury is Eric Bergeson's sixth book.

CPSIA information can be obtained
at www.ICGtesting.com
Printed in the USA
BVHW091454311219
568259BV00001B/1/P